The 1896 PROPHECIES

The 1896 PROPHECIES

LIZ MARTIN & BRANDON VALLORANI

with INGERSOLL LOCKWOOD

10
PREDICTIONS
of
AMERICA'S
LAST DAYS

FIDELIS
BOOKS

A FIDELIS BOOKS BOOK
An Imprint of Post Hill Press
ISBN: 979-8-88845-305-6
ISBN (eBook): 979-8-88845-306-3

The 1896 Prophecies:
10 Predictions of America's Last Days
© 2023 by Bravera Holdings, LLC
All Rights Reserved

Cover Design by Cody Corcoran

Post Hill Press
New York • Nashville
posthillpress.com

Published in the United States of America

Contents

Note from the Authors

We have determined the original work *1900 or The Last President* written by Ingersoll Lockwood in 1896 to be in the public domain, meaning that it is not subject to copyright.

The commentary, preface, introduction, and afterword authored by Liz Martin and Brandon Vallorani is subject to copyright.

Preface

—Liz Martin

"I prefer peace, but if trouble must come, let it be in my time that my children may know peace."—Thomas Paine

As you read the original text of Lockwood's cautionary allegory, you may be surprised at the number of references to situations, concepts, and conflagrations you'd find in our current events. I certainly was amazed to see that even in the 1800s, liberal thought was seeking a foothold as strongly as it is today.

Petulant diatribes against "the wealthy" from socialist liberals like Alexandra Ocasio-Cortez and Bernie Sanders are not new. In Chapter 8, you'll see a "packing of the Supreme Court," rendering it powerless for good.

You'll see railing against the Electoral College in favor of installing officials by popular vote. Riots ensue when the "common man" is not permitted whatever reparation they demand. Taxes on every action and activity run rampant, causing inflation that cripples the nation.

There is nothing new under the sun, so said the great king Solomon in Ecclesiastes.

Whatever term is given—liberal, leftist, communist, socialist, anarchist, progressive, Democrat—what remains evident is that despite the somewhat outdated language and poetic prose, we find a very disturbing realization: our great nation has been fighting this war for a long time.

If we intend to win the battle for the hearts, minds, and souls of our country's citizens, we must take heed of the somber warning found in the original work of Ingersoll Lockwood.

The somewhat prophetical, and certainly dire, description of what life would be like under such dereliction of our country's electoral process and checks and balances leads us to one conclusion: America's final stand is coming. It may be in your lifetime, or it may be in the lifetimes of your children or grandchildren.

During the events of 1896, America's degradation was stayed when William McKinley defeated William Jennings Bryan's progressive platform. I warrant that this has been a constant struggle ever since.

It's not too late, Patriots. We must be aware, and mentally armed with the knowledge that socialism can and must be battled every time it rears its ugly head, or we face losing the nation we love so dearly.

We have attempted to maintain the complete originality of Ingersoll Lockwood's *1900 or The Last President*, first published in 1896. Some punctuation, spellings, and formatting have been modified for better readability.

We have decided that the best way we can serve the reader to maximize the benefit from this book, without taking away from the story itself, is to introduce each chapter with some comments and observations to help the reader fully grasp details of historical context that have faded in the century since it was written, as well as how those allegorical situations correspond to circumstances we find ourselves wrestling with today.

Stantes pro deo et patria!
Liz Martin

Introduction

The little book you hold in your hand has been called "prophetic" by some.

It isn't because it unlocks some great spiritual mystery of the faith or because it gives the names and dates of great events in history. It has been called that for a different reason.

More than a century after it was written, people are struck by the similarities of predictions the author made in his book to events of our modern day.

To be fair, the author, who had not yet witnessed the dawning of the 20th century when he penned these words, never set out to describe the world as you and I would know it today. He set out on a far more modest project.

When he saw the direction the Democratic Party was taking, the people who were taking up positions of influence there, the party platform, and the now-famous speech made by their nominee, Lockwood wrote this book as a warning.

However likable and genuine he may have seemed at the time, electing a man like William Jennings Bryan to the presidency held serious real-world implications.

Lockwood's predictions were never put to the test in his lifetime because, of course, William McKinley defeated Bryan in the general election.

But the progressive ideas Bryan embodied filtered into the national bloodstream. The disposition of Americans both in our love of freedom and our commitment to the faith and ideals on which we were founded kept Bryan's ideas from gaining traction here for a very long time.

But the world has changed and changed again. Today, the Cold War is over, China has become a global power, and many of our institutions have been hijacked by cultural Marxists. Even once-reliable bulwarks against the Left's agenda like Christian faith and belief in the American Dream don't have nearly the same cultural influence they did just a few decades ago.

The ideas, the issues, and the warnings written in a book more than one hundred years ago are suddenly very much alive again and have been thrown back into national debate.

We think of Orwell and Huxley as being, in a sense, *prophetic* because of how they described the ways in which totalitarians would control the people either through fear or through entertainment and distraction.

We see how dystopian writers predicted a world in which nothing we did would be hidden from the watchful eyes of the state. We saw how science would be weaponized against our own humanity, and language would be weaponized against our ability to think independently. Ray Bradbury wrote of book burnings, predicting thought control and cancel culture. Nonconformists would be the enemy.

But these weren't prophecies, really. They were just an extrapolation of known trends being carried forward into a foreseeable future.

We saw the same thing happening with not one, but two stories written that each predicted, with shocking precision, the events surrounding the sinking of the *Titanic*.

Neither author consciously set out to write a story about one of history's great maritime disasters. Instead, they took their understanding of a straightforward problem—in this case the number of lifeboats on ocean-going ships compared to the total number of passengers and crew—and played out a realistic what-if scenario of a disaster at sea.

W. T. Stead and Morgan Robertson both told harrowing tales of a ship going down after hitting an iceberg in the North Atlantic, with many perishing needlessly.

Morgan Robertson, author of *The Wreck of the Titan*, obviously knew a thing or two about sailing. He came remarkably close to the truth with his dimensions of the ship, and the conditions that led to the ship's sinking. The fictional ship's name was a natural enough choice for the "largest ship ever made," but the similarity is still hard to overlook. Some of his more superstitious contemporaries were convinced he was a clairvoyant.

The book you now hold was written more than fifteen years before the sinking of the *Titanic*, but modern readers will note with some interest that this book opens with a very vivid metaphor of a ship slamming into an iceberg. For a book whose predictive power is being compared to that of Stead and Robertson, it's an interesting irony.

The interest in this book has generated is due, in part, to the fact that this is not the only book written by this author.

The fact that the title character in one of his novels is Baron Trump—nearly the same name as the forty-fifth president's son—was too delicious a coincidence for many to overlook.

Others have suggested that this book was, in some sense, a prediction of Trump's own presidency disrupting the status quo, and much was made about events in the opening chapter seemingly occurring at what later became Trump Tower. (The two locations were pretty close, but the events in the story unfolded at an address several blocks away.)

A fair reading of the content does not describe anything like a Trump presidency. How could it be since Trump ran as a conservative? It *does*, however, describe the very socialist influences whose takeover of America he was working so hard to oppose.

What was the author of this book trying to accomplish?

The easiest explanation would be to set it in a modern context. This book was written in 1896, after the Democrats had chosen their nominee, and after that nominee, William Jennings Bryan had both given his "Cross of Gold" speech and the Democrats had published their Chicago platform of that year.

Bryan had allied himself with his generation's answer to the Bernie Sanders/Alexandria Ocasio-Cortez socialist wing of his party and was pledging to pull his party hard to the Left in an appeal to "the common man."

The easiest way for us to see this book in its proper context is to imagine an alternate history in which the DNC did not put its thumb on the scale to help Hillary defeat Bernie for the DNC nomination in 2016.

Imagine the party establishment lining up behind him and writing their platform based on his promises and the private agendas of some billionaire backers who think they can leverage his movement for their own gain.

Picture a modern patriot being absolutely horrified with what a Bernie presidency could mean for America, and him writing a short novel—complete with the all-too-familiar names and political players of today—in which that author shows us what happens if our country gets slammed by a "democratic socialist" American presidency.

Maybe the country doesn't sink into chaos the very second it hits that metaphorical iceberg, but the clock is ticking.

That's exactly the project Ingersoll Lockwood took on with *1900 or The Last President.*

While they may no longer have significance to us, the people, issues, and political questions of the day to which he refers would all have been recognizable to anyone in that election cycle who read the daily newspapers and followed politics.

It's easy to forget what Lockwood was up against. When he was writing this, he was up against the energy of a new idea that claimed it could solve an old problem, and a real one. It promised to ease the suffering of the masses. It seemed to be anchored in compassion and love of the common man—a theme we'll see again and again in this book.

At a time when America was just climbing out of the Long Depression, this new ideology promised to make sure nobody did without. The weight of these promises would fall, they say, on those who were strong enough to bear the load.

Lockwood didn't have the modern reference points we have. He couldn't look at the failures in Venezuela, Zimbabwe, or Maoist China, or the atrocities committed against their own people by Lenin and Stalin in the USSR. Lenin's revolution was still a generation away. The Communist Party now ruling China wasn't even formed until 1921.

The author saw the rise in socialist-aligned anarchist movements, and the leading "progressive" figures of his day like John Peter Altgeld. He could look across the Atlantic at the influence of Marx on other countries and see an ugly trend forming. It took some real insight to look at the events and really understand what they meant for the rest of us.

There were a lot of ways he could have gotten his message out. Why did he choose to put it as a story?

Whether you are talking about the 19th century or the 21st, the ideas embodied in "Make America Great Again" and the wild promises of "Build Back Better" are in conflict. They cannot *both* be true. But, as buyers' remorse in the Biden presidency is proving, you can't just take political ideas for a test drive and then return them if they don't work out. In politics, all sales are final.

But stories are a safe place to let ideas run free and to see how the experiment ends. Even Jesus used stories—parables—to get ideas across. Why?

Because unlike an essay, a story engages the mind, the imagination, and the emotions. By being immersive, it lets you "see" what's happening in a much richer way. You can feel a story where commentary might merely engage the mind.

The references, of course, are dated, and the world has changed dramatically from the time it was written. Some things—like the depiction of racial minorities in his day (which was, incidentally, the same year *Plessy v. Ferguson* was decided)—may seem foreign or even shocking to our modern ears.

But in the broad strokes, *The Last President*'s warning remains just as fresh and relevant today as it was when first written. And there is a reason for that.

It was never a story about just one man. It was really about the ideas with which he was trying to "fundamentally transform" both America and our economy. Ideas that are all too familiar to anyone who has been paying attention to the competing visions of the increasingly hard-Left Obama and Biden administrations on one side and Trump's "Make America Great Again" movement on the other.

Trump boldly pledged in his 2019 State of the Union address that America would never be a socialist country. The Democrats, meanwhile, have been using every tool at their disposal to try and prove him wrong.

Reagan once warned that we are never more than one generation away from losing our freedom. This political conflict between collectivist socialism on the Left and rugged American individualism on the Right is nothing new.

The seeds of it were already germinating at the close of the 19th century. We dodged a bullet then, and perhaps, with the help of his warning, Americans can do so again.

Commentary on Chapter 1

Lockwood was able to squeeze an entire world of ideas into ten slim chapters because he was drawing from a wealth of shared experience and knowledge of contemporaries in his own day.

His book was written during the election cycle of 1896, after the nominees were chosen, but before the vote was cast. (Based on clues from the plot itself, it was most likely published before September.) It was written with one intent—to address the critical issues of his day.

Instead of writing a dreary series of essays with laborious facts, figures, and citations that would be generally ignored and quickly forgotten, he wrapped his reflections and insights in a message that would engage not just the mind, but the imagination and emotions of the reader as well. (There's a lesson in there for would-be pundits of our own day.)

Like Scrooge in Dickens's classic *A Christmas Carol*, the reader is taken into the presidency as it *might* be, with an implicit warning that unless he takes the better path, what lies ahead will be filled with sorrow and regret.

Readers from the 19th century would need no explanation of what was driving the contentious issues of their day. Those issues and the personalities behind them would have regularly featured in contemporary headlines have been long since forgotten by the generations that followed.

It's only natural for someone writing to his own generation to skip those cultural and contextual explanations, isn't it?

If someone 120 years from now were to pick up a book describing events around the 2016 and 2020 elections, they might have some sense of the red state/blue state conflict, but they might be baffled about how those elections had been impacted by events, movements, cultural artifacts, and personalities that are all too familiar to the rest of us.

It's easy to take for granted all the topics people today could jump straight into that might leave readers a century from now scratching their heads.

Here are just a few such details we might reference in a story chronicling the Trump years in no particular order: "Bernie Bros," Jim Acosta, "mean tweets," the financial influence of George Soros and Planned Parenthood, Jim Comey, pink-hatted marchers, Facebook memes, Pepe the Frog, the alt-Right, Breitbart, bathroom rights, Bruce/Caitlyn Jenner, various "-phobias" and "-isms," black-bloc rioters breaking windows and burning down Starbucks, Antifa, school shootings, *Macedonian Content Farmers*, the Steele dossier and "Russian collusion," the unexpected death of Justice Scalia, and the failed appointment of Merrick Garland.

The items on this list may mean something to us (if we haven't already forgotten), but future readers coming across those same ideas would be left with more questions than answers.

For all the fame and power they may have enjoyed in their lifetimes, even figures whose prominence we now take for granted will have long since faded into distant memory. Nancy Pelosi, Chuck Schumer, Michael Avenatti, Anthony Fauci, Mitch McConnell, Rush Limbaugh, John McCain, Antony Blinken, George Floyd, Hunter Biden, Joe Rogan, Harvey Weinstein,

Tara Reade, and many others would need context and footnotes before they could be understood.

Without the backdrop of environmentalism, identity politics, the rising influence of "the Squad," and the brand of socialism that was well on its way to capturing most of our political and cultural institutions, any future reader couldn't even begin to fully grasp those two elections.

They don't even touch the immediate questions raised by the disagreements on how to respond to concerns of Islamic terrorism, illegal immigration, and economic policy in the 2016 election, or questions of COVID mandates or BLM riots in 2020.

But since his short story only has ten chapters, he's not slowing down for any of those details. As Lockwood skips right to the chase and begins with the election result, you can almost imagine his writing flying off the blocks in answer to a starter's pistol.

Boom.

It's Election Day in November of 1896. The Democrat had squeaked out an unlikely win, and all hell is breaking loose in the big city. Good citizens are told to "shelter in place" while a riotous mob floods the streets of New York declaring its triumph.

New York's finest are doing their best to beat back the mob, but facing exhaustion and superior numbers, they are losing ground and their line is in danger of breaking completely.

Reinforcements come; there is a military clash with the anarchists in the street and the dead anarchists are carried away in wagons, with an ominous quote from the governor to end the chapter in answer to the relief of the city being saved: "Aye, but the republic…."

Why would Election Day begin with riots? It has everything to do with who the Democrat candidate really was.

The man who took the Democratic nomination in 1896 was exactly the kind of candidate behind whom the likes of Bernie Sanders or Alexandria Ocasio-Cortez could have thrown their fullest support.

These were the early days of what eventually came to be known as the progressive movement (or, as Mark Levin has accurately dubbed it, "American Marxism").

This was in the Gilded Age. It was a time overflowing with optimism about the possibilities of human potential. New theories were abundant, and a breathless public was anxious to put them into practice. The West was being tamed, slavery had been ended, and America was trying to come to grips with what sort of a country it was to become going forward.

While this was a time of amazing opportunity for some, the working class kept working hard jobs and long hours. They started taking issue with how they were treated by their employers, some of whom really were badly exploiting their own workers.

We were already seeing the beginnings of labor action—this was only ten years after the Haymarket Affair—and an air of revolution was already in the air throughout the world. A radical leftist faction called the Fabian Society had spread up in the 1800s, offering a flavor of Marxism that worked to capture and transform society rather than openly declaring a bloody revolution.

Political movements were reacting to what they saw as a problem that needed to be solved: there was an enormous wealth gap between the haves and the have-nots, and there was only one explanation they would accept for how something like that can happen. Rich people had exploited poor people to get rich off of their labor.

Once you have been convinced that criminal exploitation is the only explanation for how they could have gotten rich, the corrective measures—which will be necessarily draconian and authoritarian—become self-evident.

If the wealthy have no right to their wealth, it is a simple matter of justice, and definitely not a sin, to take it from them.

As we later saw through the entire 20th century, a whole range of unspeakably evil actions can take place, as soon as those with power to act have convinced themselves those actions are justifiable. What is true at the individual level is no less true of nations or cultures, or organizations.

We ourselves watched as some of our own politicians and media personalities gave an energetic defense of neighborhoods being burned to the ground and police or federal buildings being attacked by mobs through the summer of 2020.

So long as it was the *right* protest for the *right* cause, even felonies like looting are waved away as *justifiable under the circumstances.*

Our own bizarre habit of selective outrage reserved for the media's approved enemy is something worth keeping in mind the next time we ask ourselves, "How did ordinary Germans tolerate the rise of the Nazi Party? How could they look the other way?"

Which brings us back to the 1890s, where the seeds of the progressive movement were just beginning to sprout and the Left's preferred language of representing the "common man" started to pick up steam.

This picks up another thread that the late 1800s and early 1900s had in common with the serious changes ushered in by social media, changes that were crystalized in the rise of President Donald Trump.

In a word, populism.

Going by objective measurements like policies he passed in his first year, Trump was incredibly mainstream in his conservative policies, having checked off 64 percent of the Heritage Foundation's wish list in his first year, compared with Reagan's 49 percent.

But anyone paying attention will notice he managed to draw support from the most unlikely of demographics—the Bernie Bro voter. Why?

It's simple—Right and Left is not the only dynamic that interests voters. There was a different problem of the demands of the well-heeled coastal elites, pulling in a different direction than the demands of the working class. The demands of the coastal elites just happened to align with the donor classes, and the media pundit classes on whose whims so many political careers depended, and concerns of the regular working stiff were forgotten in the process.

Trump and Bernie differed in many ways, but both recognized that there are a lot more working-class people than there are elites, and each citizen gets only one vote. Had Democrats not scrambled to rig the game against Bernie, we might have seen a Trump/Sanders election not once, but twice.

Populism, in some sense, is about making a direct appeal to the general population and promising to be the one to represent their interests.

There are two very different ways to embody that promise.

The Bernie Bro approach—like that of the newly-minted President Bryan in this story—is to pander to the people and promise them an abundance of free stuff at someone else's expense.

The "Make America Great Again" method is to attack red tape and regulations, reduce taxation, and have the government step out of the way so Americans can go about the business of life, liberty, and the pursuit of happiness.

When you look at the rioters turned loose in chapter 1, they look an awful lot like the rioters we saw on the news through four years of the Trump presidency. They are consumed with contempt for the wealthy and want to destroy people different from themselves.

And if they are fighting for the common man as they claim to be, why are ordinary people living in fear of their unrestrained violence, both in the opening chapter of this book and in the modern world?

These rioters voted for socialism, and they were going to get it—good and hard.

In the coming chapters, we'll take a closer look at specific policies and personnel that played a role in shaping the battle to win the White House in 1896.

1

Election Day Shocker

That was a terrible night for the great city of New York—the night of Tuesday, November 3rd, 1896. The city staggered under the blow like a huge ocean liner which plunges, full speed, with terrific crash into a mighty iceberg, and recoils shattered and trembling like an aspen.

The people were gathered, light-hearted and confident, at the evening meal, when the news burst upon them. It was like a thunder bolt out of an azure sky:

"Altgeld holds Illinois hard and fast in the Democratic line. This elects Bryan president of the United States!"

Strange to say, the people in the upper portion of the city made no movement to rush out of their houses and collect in the public squares, although the night was clear and beautiful. They sat as if paralyzed with a nameless dread, and when they conversed it was with bated breath and throbbing hearts.

In less than half an hour, mounted policemen dashed through the streets calling out:

"Keep within your houses; close your doors and barricade them. The entire East side is in a state of uproar. Mobs of vast size are organizing under the lead of anarchists and socialists and threaten to plunder and despoil the houses of the rich who have wronged and oppressed them for so many years. Keep within doors. Extinguish all lights."

Happily, Governor Morton was in town, and although a deeper pallor overcame the ashen hue of age as he spoke, there was no tremor in his voice:

"Let the Seventh, Twenty-Second and Seventy-First regiments be ordered under arms." In a few moments, hundreds of messengers could be heard racing through the silent streets, summoning the members of these regiments to their armories.

Slowly, but with astonishing nerve and steadiness, the mobs pushed the police northward, and although the force stood the onslaught with magnificent courage, yet beaten back, the dark masses of infuriated beings surged up again with renewed fury and strength.

Will the troops be in time to save the city? Was the whispered inquiry among the knots of police officials who were directing the movements of their men.

About nine o'clock, with deafening outcries, the mob, like a four-headed monster breathing fire and flame, raced, tore, burst, raged into Union Square.

The police force was exhausted, but their front was still like a wall of stone save that it was movable. The mob crowded it steadily to the north, while the air quivered and was rent with mad vociferations of the victor:

"Bryan is elected! Bryan is elected! Our day has come at last. Down with our oppressors! Death to the rich man! Death to the gold bungs! Death to the capitalists! Give us back the money you have ground out of us. Give us back the marrow of our bones which you have used to grease the wheels of your chariots!"

The police force was now almost helpless. The men still used their sticks, but the blows were ineffectual, and only served to increase the rage of the vast hordes now advancing upon Madison Square.

The Fifth Avenue Hotel will be the first to feel the fury of the mob. Would the troops be in time to save it?

A half cheer, a half cry of joy goes up. It is inarticulate. Men draw a long breath; women drop upon their knees and strain their eyes; they can hear something, but they cannot see as yet, for the gas houses and electric plants had been destroyed by the mob early in the evening. They preferred to fight in the dark, or by the flames of rich men's abodes.

Again a cheer goes up, louder and clearer this time, followed by cries of "They're coming, they're coming."

Yes, they were coming—the Twenty-Second down Broadway, the Seventh down Madison Avenue, both on the double quick.

In a moment or so there were a few bugle calls, and a few spoken commands rang out clear and sharp; and then the two regiments stretched across the entire square, literally from wall to wall, in line of battle. The mob was upon them. Would this slender line of troops, could it hold such a mighty mass of men in check?

The answer was a deafening discharge of firearms, a terrific crack, such as some thunder bolts make when they explode. A wall of fire blazed across the Square. Again and again it blazed forth. The mob halted, stood fast, wavered, fell back, advanced again.

At that moment there came a rattle as of huge knives in the distance.

It was the gallant Seventy-First charging up Twenty-Third Street and taking the mob on the flank. They came on like a wall of iron, bristling with blades of steel.

There were no outcries, no cheers from the regiment. It dealt out death in silence, save when two bayonets crossed and clashed in bearing down some doubly vigorous foe.

As the bells rang out midnight, the last remnants of the mob were driven to cover, but the wheels of the dead wagons rattled till daybreak.

And then the aged governor, in response to the mayor's "Thank God, we've saved the city!" made the answer:

"Aye, but the republic...."

Commentary on Chapter 2

A lot can change in a hundred years...and (in some ways), it really has.

For us to really understand the plot in this book, we have to step back through time to the world in which it was written.

We now live in a world of space flight and GPS, of nanotech and gene splicing, of iPhones and just-in-time supply-chain management. We live in a world handed down to us by the heroes of two world wars, and the sacrifice of Civil War leaders.

We have split the atom and survived a Cold War between nuclear-capable powers. Even our highway system was still a distant dream when the book you are holding was first written. This was, after all, the year Henry Ford first tested his gasoline-powered engine on a "quadricycle."

For us to understand the world in which this book was written, we will need to look around at the context of the day.

To Lockwood's readers, Abraham Lincoln wasn't the distant historical figure he has since become. Remembering him was analogous to this generation reminiscing about Ronald Reagan. Those who lived through those times would still be able to tell stories to younger people who came after. But there were many who could still remember him firsthand.

The Second World War is another historical benchmark that can help us calibrate the timeline. For the sake of round numbers, let's use the seventy-five-year gap between the end of World War II and 2020. The eighty-four-year gap between when

1900 or The Last President was written, and the War of 1812 is not far off from that timescale.

Their generation's historical memory of Napoleon was about the same as our memory of Hitler and Stalin.

Let's go a little further and anchor ourselves in the events of 1896 itself.

What happened in that year? Utah had just become the forty-fifth state, the first radio transmission was made, and X-rays were discovered. Miami became incorporated as a city. SCOTUS made its infamous *Plessy v. Ferguson* ruling. The first modern Olympiad was held. Charles Dow published the first Dow Jones Industrial Average. And lastly, America didn't know it yet, but the early dominoes triggering the Spanish-American War were already starting to tumble.

With the modern use of paper money—not to mention plastic or digital—the passion anyone could throw behind arcane questions of coinage, the Mint, the gold standard or bimetallism, and income tax seem strange to our modern ears. As for income tax, it would be almost twenty more years before that forever changed how the country paid its bills.

If you have physical silver, should you have the right to melt it down into coins or not? Is inflation a good thing or a bad thing? If you think printing money is a new problem, it isn't. That question looms as large in this book as it does in today's politics.

The economic role of silver becomes the lynchpin question to understanding the central conflict in this book. There was a question over whether the banks and the government should control the money supply, or if every citizen should have the right to bring the silver they have at home to a mint and have it made into coins.

A close reading of this book shows it was written as a critical response to the Democratic candidate's famous "Cross of Gold" speech at the DNC on July 9, 1896, and the Chicago platform that came out from that same DNC. The short story you now hold in your hands picks up on Bryan's platform and imagines what might become of a society that tries to put those ill-conceived ideas into practice.

The silver policy itself will be covered in a later chapter, but the party politics behind that divide are very relevant in this chapter.

Silver was a populist cause that was picked up by early progressives, and that shines a light on why New York (still a Republican-leaning, business-focused state at that point in our history) had such a different response to the election in the first chapter than Chicago did in the second chapter.

Rioters ran rampant in New York because to them, this was a show of strength and of regime change. The progressives had won, and this was a way of laying claim to their prize after winning.

A similar pattern of burning and looting could just as easily have shown up in social media feeds during the Trump years, and especially during the 2020 election cycle—right up until the moment that Biden fans on CNN started wondering out loud if these riots were hurting Democrat polling numbers.

Why would the same election that caused rioters to burn and loot in Lockwood's imagining of New York City on Election Day react so differently in this second chapter?

Then, as now, the answer can be found by looking at Chicago politics. In particular, it can be found by looking at the man often referenced but never actually named in this chapter.

His name is not given, but we learn a lot from the titles he is given: "the master spirit" that kept the mobs "in leash"; "conqueror"; "Kingmaker"; the "Savior" who has "cleaned the Temple of Liberty"; and the man that even the newly minted President Bryan would call "Master."

This unnamed man would have "his reward," would "stand behind the throne," and his wisdom would "make us whole." With misplaced religious zeal, the crowds declared themselves "slaves" to this shadow figure who was to be elevated above Washington, Lincoln, or Grant.

There's a clue to his identity in the depiction of when the boisterous crowd fell upon and murdered four federal soldiers in their glee.

"…and so they died, four brave men clad in the blue livery of the republic whose only crime was that some months back, against the solemn protest of the master, their comrades had set foot on the soil of the commonwealth and saved the metropolis of the West from the hands of this same mob."

What significant event happened in Chicago "some months back" from Election Day of 1896?

How about the Pullman Strike of 1894? A workers' strike against labor practices by a rail company quickly snowballed out of control, grinding rail traffic—not to mention mail and commerce—to a halt. Thirty people were killed in the Chicago riots alone. More were killed elsewhere in the country.

Restoring order to Chicago took President Cleveland sending federal troops, but the governor of Illinois was not happy about it. John Peter Altgeld (1847–1902) had very clear prolabor leanings and—though a foreign-born German socialist—a surprising amount of influence in the U.S. politics of the day.

What do we know about Altgeld and the kind of influence he brought to American politics?

For one thing, he leaned all the way into the idea of being a "man of the people," which won him a great deal of support at a moment in American history in which the economy had been slumping for a long time. This ties back into the Long Depression, a drop in the value of silver, and the Coinage Act of 1873, which makes an appearance in a later chapter.

He had something of a mixed legacy. His child-labor laws and workplace safety were groundbreaking. He appointed women to positions of influence, and he poured money into public education. His attitude to law enforcement would be welcomed by today's Soros-backed DAs, as he pardoned 108 people of various crimes in his four-year term, including nineteen convicted murderers. Local papers called him John "Pardon" Altgeld.

He has the dubious distinction of being considered "synonymous with the dawn of the Progressive era," according to historian Philip Drey. Supporters had nicknamed him "the poor man's friend."

But let's look at what made Altgeld famous. For someone who only served as governor for four years, he certainly made the most of it.

It started with his treatment of the surviving bombers from the Haymarket Affair of 1886, in which a labor protest became a riot when someone from the crowd threw a bomb at the police. Eight people died in the violence of that day, and several of those charged for conspiracy were later hanged for it.

While labor protests were raised against real indignities being suffered by the workers, socialist movements were happy to leverage those legitimate feelings of angst to raise the profile of their revolutionary agenda. What did Altgeld do? He pardoned those who had been convicted of the bombing, claiming the system had been unfairly rigged against them. It's not exactly the same as Kamala Harris raising bail for those who looted and burned their way through the summer of 2020, but it's close enough.

Altgeld got a name for himself as a "friend of the common man" in his ongoing support of labor movements. The right saw him as a friend of someone else—the revolutionary movement.

Altgeld was seen from that time forward as a friend of anarchists and socialists...not unlike a certain junior senator Democrat from Illinois whose trek to the White House began in the Chicago living room of a former Weather Underground terrorist.

Maybe that explains why Grover Cleveland didn't ask Altgeld's permission before quelling the Pullman Strike rioting in 1894. He would have been refused just as resolutely as blue states and DC refused Trump's offer of the National Guard to quell rioters.

History looked favorably on Cleveland's decisiveness that day.

Altgeld saw Cleveland as antilabor and used his considerable national influence to drive the Democrats away from Cleveland's orbit. Altgeld was committed to the cause of silver, and, before the history in this book transitioned into the realm of fiction, it had been Altgeld's support in the fifth ballot after Bryan's "Cross of Gold" speech that elevated Bryan to become the Democrats' official nominee.

Contemporary accounts of Altgeld in the context of this election don't mince words.

Teddy Roosevelt was harsh. *Harper's Weekly* was savage. Both of the following quotes were from October of 1896. Here's Roosevelt's opinion of the man:

> Mr. Altgeld is a much more dangerous man than Bryan. He is much slyer, much more intelligent, much less silly, much more free from all the restraints of public morality. The one is unscrupulous from vanity, the other from calculation. The one plans wholesale repudiation with a light heart and bubbly eloquence because he lacks intelligence...the other would connive at wholesale murder and would justify it by elaborate and cunning sophistry for reasons known only to his own tortuous soul. For America to put men like this in control of her destiny would be such a dishonor as it is scarcely bearable to think of.

And this was *Harper's Weekly*:

> Governor Altgeld...is the brains and inspiration of the movement for which Mr. Bryan stands.... It is he who chose Mr. Bryan in preference to Mr. Bland.... Governor Altgeld preferred the impulsive, susceptible, imaginative, yielding Mr. Bryan...who would be as clay in the hands of the potter under the astute control of the ambitious and unscrupulous Illinois communist.... To Governor Altgeld the passage of a law establishing free coinage of silver would be but a

> step towards the general socialism which is the fundamental doctrine of his political belief.... He seeks to overturn the old parties, the old traditions, and the essential policies which have controlled the government since its foundation.

Coming back to the central question—why would 1896 Chicago escape the wrath of rioters when New York did not? Because rioting would hurt the political cause so desired by those seeking power, rather than help it.

Remember that *Time Magazine* story where a whole range of unlikely groups—including protesters, business, media, and others—worked together to "fortify" the election for Joe Biden? Suddenly, the BLM rioters melted right away, even as they circulated pledges to "become ungovernable" if the "wrong" guy were to win that 2020 election.

It's a tacit admission that these acts of violence are little more than the militant wing of the Democratic Party...and over the intervening century between then and now, not much has changed.

2

CHAPTER

Meanwhile, in Chicago...

Great as has been the world's wonder at the uprising of Mr. Bryan's "struggling masses" in the city by the sea, and the narrow escape of its magnificent homes from fire and brand, yet greater still was the wonderment when the news was flashed across the land that Chicago did not stand in need of a single federal soldier.

"Chicago is made, but it is the madness of joy. Chicago is in the hands of the mob, but it is a mob made up of her own people—noisy, rude and boisterous, the natural exultation of a suddenly enfranchised class; but bent on no other mischief than glorying over the villainous and self-seeking souls who have ground the faces of the poor and turned the pitiless screw of social and political power into the hearts of the common people until its last thread had been reached, and despair pressed its lupine visage hard against the door of the laboring man."

And yet, at this moment when the night air quivered with the mad vociferations of the "common people," that the Lord had been good to them; that the wicked money changers had been driven from the temple, that the stony-hearted usurers were beaten at last, that the "People's William" was at the helm now, that peace and plenty would in a few moons come back to the poor man's cottage, that silver was king, aye, king at last, the world still went wondering why red-eyed anarchy, as she stood in Haymarket Square, with thin arms aloft, with wild mien and wilder gesticulation, drew no bomb of dynamite from her bosom, to hurl at the hated minions of the law who were silent spectators of this delirium of popular joy.

Why was it thus? Look and you shall know why white-robed peace kept step with this turbulent band and turned its thought from red-handed pillage. He was there. The master spirit to hold them in leash.

He, and he alone, had lifted Bryan to his great eminence. Without these twenty-four electoral votes, Bryan had been doomed, hopelessly doomed. He, and he alone, held the great commonwealth of the West hard and fast in the Democratic line; hence he came as conqueror, as Kingmaker, and the very walls of the sky-touching edifices trembled as he was dragged through the crowded streets by this orderly mob, and ten times ten thousand of his creatures bellowed his name and shook their hats aloft in mad exultation:

"You're our Savior, you've cleaned the Temple of Liberty of its foul horde of usurers. We salute you. We call you Kingmaker. Bryan shall call you Master too. You shall have your reward. You shall stand behind the throne. Your wisdom shall make us whole. You shall purge the land of this unlawful crowd of money lenders. You shall save the republic. You are greater than Washington. You're a better friend of ours than Lincoln. You'll do more for us than Grant. We're your slaves. We salute you. We thank you. We bless you. Hurrah! Hurrah! Hurrah!"

But yet this vast throng of tamed monsters, this mighty mob of momentarily good-natured haters of established order, broke away from the master's control for a few brief moments and dipped their hands in the enemy's blood.

The deed was swift as it was terrible. There were but four of them, unarmed, on pleasure bent. At sight of these men, a thousand throats belched out a deep and awful growl of hatred.

They were brave men and backed against the wall to die like brave men, stricken down, beaten, torn, trampled, dragged, it was quick work. They had faced howling savages in the far West, painted monsters in human form, but never had they heard such yells leave the throats of men; and so they died, four brave men, clad in the blue livery of the republic, whose only crime was that some months back, against the solemn protest of the Master, their comrades had set foot on the soil of the commonwealth, and saved the metropolis of the West from the hands of this same mob.

And so Chicago celebrated the election of the new president who was to free the land from the grasp of the moneylenders and undo the bad business of years of unholy union between barterers and sellers of human toil and the law makers of the land.

Throughout the length and breadth of the South, and beyond the Great Divide, the news struck hamlet and village like the glad tidings of a new evangel, almost as potent for human happiness as the heavenly message of two thousand years ago.

Bells rang out in joyful acclaim, and the very stars trembled at the telling, and the telling over and over of what had been done for the poor man by his brethren of the North, and around the blazing pine knots of the Southern cabin and in front of the mining camp fires of the Far West, the cry went up:

15

"Silver is King! Silver is King!"

Black palms and white were clasped in this strange love-feast, and the dark-skinned grandchild no longer felt the sting of the lash on his sire's shoulder.

All was peace and goodwill, for the people were at last victorious over their enemies who had taxed and tithed them into a very living death.

Now the laborer would not only be worthy of his hire, but it would be paid to him in a people's dollar, for the people's good, and now the rich man's coffers would be made to yield up their ill-gotten gain, and the sun would look upon this broad and fair land and find no man without a market for the product of his labors.

Henceforth, the rich man should, as was right and proper, pay a royal sum for the privilege of his happiness, and take the nation's taxes on his broad shoulders, where they belong.

Commentary on Chapter 3

It doesn't take a landslide victory to change the course of history, especially in America. Just look at the Biden presidency.

Pelosi held the narrowest margin the House had seen in a long time. The Senate didn't even produce a majority. It was deadlocked except for the fact that Harris' position as veep placed the gavel in Chuck Schumer's hands. But as we all saw, the lack of any clear mandate didn't stop them from cranking the wheel hard to the left and driving the country into a ditch.

In Lockwood's book, we see the same dynamic playing out. Bryan's election was not a landslide in any sense of the word. He tells us in no uncertain terms that it took Illinois to put him over the top in the Electoral College. But because Bryan took the House and Senate too, his party's control of all three would soon be enough to drastically alter the course of American history.

Only SCOTUS now had power to stand between Bryan and his goals, and with a few appointments, even that would soon change.

For the next four years, a coalition of Bryan's populists and the Free Silver men would hold sway in dictating how the nation was to be run.

The initial tension of those Election Day riots passed quickly. Now, the nation anxiously held its breath and waited for the day when President Grover Cleveland would yield the White House to his successor, William Jennings Bryan.

Whether you saw that changing of the guard as deliverance or doom would depend on whether Bryan's campaign had delivered you promises or threats. The bankers and the businessmen well understood the financial beatings that would be waiting for them. But those who had elected him waited with anticipation for the dawning of a new day.

In the time of that anticipation, those to whom Bryan's campaign had most directly appealed began daydreaming about all the promises they had been given. Many neglected the ordinary duties of their lives and got wrapped up in discussions about the politics of the day and the big changes that would be coming.

Those conversations about politics, and the election itself, had been heavily influenced by the recent Panic of 1893. To make the long story short, political upheaval in Argentina had ripple effects impacting North America, which led to people pulling money out of the banks, which triggered a lending crunch, bankruptcies, and so on. Investors retreated to gold as a safe haven and waited for the crisis to blow over.

In that time, almost one in four rail companies went into receivership. The infamous Pullman Strike in Chicago, which led to riots both there and around the country, came to a boil in the midst of this crisis.

Falling prices were hurting farmers, and there were more than four million unemployed. For anyone already living on the margins, ordinary Americans whose pride would normally have kept them from ever entertaining such options turned to newly opened soup kitchens. Even some ordinary housewives and mothers were reportedly reduced to prostitution.

This is how "Coxey's Army" enters our story.

For those of us used to seeing demonstrations of hundreds of thousands of people descending on Washington, D.C., to make their voices heard, we might skip right over the significance of just how groundbreaking this moment was in American history.

It's easy to forget, when something like that has become "routine," how jarring the impact must have been the first time it happened. They would have been even more jarring than the Canadian Truckers' Protests of 2022 in the sense that there had been no precedent with which to compare it.

What might have been the very first march on Washington came as a response to the hard times in 1894 we have been describing.

Jacob S. Coxey was an Ohio businessman who saw the people in distress and proposed a solution that will be instantly recognizable to the modern reader. He proposed an "infrastructure program" to get people back to work.

He called his group the United States Industrialized Army and gained support for his project in an unorthodox way. He organized a "petition in boots," and the news of his project gained support among the unemployed from around the country. Maybe four hundred of the original participants made the full five-week trip to Washington. Some from other parts of the country were turned back.

On May 1, 1894, the remaining marchers arrived at the Capitol building. Police tried to turn them away, but they had come to be heard. Coxey and others climbed the fence and were arrested for—would you believe—*trespassing on the Capitol lawn*.

Although Coxey's Army's demands were not met immediately, some of the ideas Coxey presented would eventually be adopted in the 20th century, as we have witnessed.

Lockwood intuitively understood that Coxey had now struck a bell that could never be unrung. A precedent had been set with crowds flowing into D.C. to have their voices heard. We will see this new tactic make an appearance more than once in his book.

As modern readers will know in hindsight, no single party or issue has had a monopoly on that democratic tool for petitioning their government. Some of our greatest moments have centered around such marches. Some of our most righteous causes have been taken up on the lips of such crowds. But as recent and less honorable instances of burning and looting have reminded us, it's a tool indifferent to any question of morality. It can just as easily be used for good as for evil.

In the third chapter, because of grandiose election promises that had been made, some of the "common" people to whom Bryan had appealed were convinced that all they needed to do was show up in D.C. and a world of new opportunity would be waiting there for them.

Among those grandiose promises was one about citizens having a right to the minting of their silver into dollar coins and doing so at a standardized ratio to gold values. This came at a moment in history where new mines in the western states meant America was suddenly flush with silver—a wave of "Silver Pilgrims" were encouraged to follow the example of Coxey's Army and descend en masse upon the Capitol to await help from on high.

Con men, as will always be the case, took advantage of their naivety and optimism, selling them all kinds of "silverware" for them to take with them to melt down for money. Naturally, the silverware they'd been sold was a fraud and only silver-plated.

But by the time the victims realized that, the con men would be long gone and looking for new victims.

Con men weren't the only people taking advantage of genuinely down-and-out common people looking for a fresh start. As we still see today, there were "community organizers" who had gathered these "armies" together. Was it because of care and concern for their needs? Not according to Lockwood. These "leaders" were interested only in harnessing this movement as an opportunity they could leverage into gaining public office.

Each of those Silver Pilgrims made their trip to Washington confident in the belief that when they arrived there, the friend of the common man would most certainly welcome them with open arms and find in his administration some manner of work suitable for them, even if that meant throwing out all the scoundrels who worked there already.

The author's understanding of term limits and throwing the bums out was nothing so radical as modern calls to drain the swamp have become. The kind of corruption he thought needed addressing was the far more pedestrian kind—issues like political careerism and nepotism.

We will see in later chapters that even Lockwood didn't foresee an America so corrupt that it would conduct large-scale political purges of people with the "wrong" political beliefs. Large-scale purges of such political enemies were still somewhere in the distant future...well, at least from *his* perspective in history, they were still a long way off.

The political implications of an education system that had been hijacked by Marxist sympathizers had yet to leave a mark on culture. Obama's large-scale purges of the military leadership had not yet run their course. Big Tech censorship and modern cancel culture had not yet reared their heads.

The chapter ends with a solemn note, remembering that other group who awaits the coming day not with joyous optimism, but with the abject horror of a man on death row.

The Reign of the People, like so many revolutions before it, would entail the new powers demonizing and toppling the old ones. Unlike the War of Independence, which cut America free of an English king, or the French Revolution, which declared war on both king and clergy, this revolution was taking aim at American commerce itself.

Having any success in Wall Street or business is suddenly proof enough that you are somehow enriching yourself by the exploitation of others.

The Silver Pilgrims' daydreams of getting hired by the new administration invoked unsettling imagery of a Roman emperor's triumphal return with the spoils of war in the closing words of the chapter.

Notably, Rich Men, Wall Street, and Corporations were named as the very denizens of Hell. These "soulless monsters" would be taken in chains behind the "silver chariot" of the conquering President Bryan, the Conqueror from the West.

And there was nothing they could do to stop it.

3

CHAPTER

The Silver Pilgrims

The pens of many writers would not suffice to describe with anything like historical fullness and precision the wild scenes of excitement which, on the morning after Election Day, burst forth on the floors of the various exchanges throughout the Union.

The larger and more important the money center, the deeper, blacker, and heavier the despair which sank upon them after the violent ebullitions of protest, defiance, and execration had subsided.

With some, it seemed that visions of their swift but sure impoverishment only served to transform the dark and dismal drama of revolution and disintegration into a side-splitting farce, and they greeted the prospective loss of their millions with loud guffaws and indescribable antics of horseplay and unseemly mirth.

As the day wore on, the news became worse and worse. It was only too apparent that the House of Representatives of the Fifty-Fifth Congress would be controlled by the combined vote of the Populists and Free Silver men, while the wild joy with which the entire South welcomed the election of Bryan and Sewall left little doubt in the mind of the Northern people that the Southern Senators would, to a man, range themselves on the administration side of the great conflict into which the republic was soon to be precipitated.

Add to these the twenty senators of the Free Silver States of the North, and the new president would have the Congress of the republic at his back. There would be nothing to stand between him and the realization of those schemes which an exuberant fancy, untamed by the hand of experience, and scornful of the leading-strings of wisdom, can conjure up.

Did we say nothing? Nay, not so; for the Supreme Court was still there. And yet Justice Field had come fully up to the eightieth milestone in the journey of life, and Justice Gray was nearly seventy, while one or two other members of this High Court of Judicature held to their lives with feeble grasp.

Even in due and orderly course of events, why might there not come vacancies and then?

In spite of the nameless dread that rested upon so many of our people, and chilled by the very blood of the country's industries, the new year '97 came hopefully, serenely, almost defiantly in.

There was an indescribable something in the air, a spirit of political devil-may-care, a feeling that the old order had passed away and that the republic had entered into the womb of time and been born again.

This sentiment began to give outward and visible signs of its existence and growth in the remote agricultural districts of the South and Far West.

They threw aside their working implements, loitered about, gathered in groups and the words Washington, White House, Silver, Bryan, Offices, Two for One, the South's Day, Reign of the Common People, Taxes, Incomes, Year of Jubilee, Free Coinage, Wall Street, Altgeld, Tillman, Peffer, Coxey, were whispered in a mysterious way with head noddings and pursings up of the mouth.

As January wore away and February, slipping by, brought Bryan's inauguration nearer and nearer, the groups melted into groups, and it was only too apparent that from a dozen different points in the South and Northwest "Coxey Armies" were forming for an advance on Washington.

In some instances they were well clad and well provisioned; in others, they were little better than great bands of hungry and restless men, demoralized by idleness and wrought up to a strange degree of mental excitement by the extravagant harangues of their leaders, who were animated with but one thought, namely, to make use of these vast crowds of Silver Pilgrims, as they called themselves, to back up their claims for public office.

These crowds of deluded people were well named "Silver Pilgrims," for hundreds of them carried in hempen bags pieces of silverware, in ninety-nine cases of a hundred, plated stuff of little value, which unscrupulous dealers and peddlers had palmed off upon them as sterling, with the promises that once in Washington, the United States Mint would coin their metal into "Bryan Dollars" giving "two for one" in payment for it.

While these motley "armies" marched upon the Capitol of the republic, the railway trains night and day brought vast crowds of "new men," politicians of low degree, men out of employment, drunken and disgruntled mechanics, farmer's sons, to seek their fortunes under the Reign of the People, heelers and hangers-on of ward bosses, old men who had not tasted office for thirty years and more, all inspired by Mr. Bryan's declaration that:

"The American people are not in favor of life tenure in the Civil Service, that a permanent office-holding class is not in harmony with our institutions, that a fixed term in appointive offices would open the public service to a larger number of citizens, without impairing its efficiency," all bearing new besoms in their hands or across their shoulders, each and every one of them supremely confident that in the distribution of the spoils something would surely fall to his share, since they were the "common people" who were so dear to Mr. Bryan, and who had made him President in the very face of the prodigious opposition of the rich men, whose coffers had been thrown wide open to all to no purpose, and in spite too of the satanic and truly devilish power of that hell upon earth known as Wall Street, which had sweated gold in vain in its desperate efforts to fasten the chains of trusts and the claws of soulless monsters known as corporations upon these very "common people," soon to march in triumph before the silver chariot of the young Conqueror from the West.

Commentary on Chapter 4

The Dawnless Day. It's easy to forget that Inauguration Day was not, as the custom now is, to take place in January.

Back in 1772, the presidential term had been established by law to begin on March 4. That custom did not change until the 20th Amendment to the Constitution was enacted before Franklin Delano Roosevelt's second term in office.

Bryan's swearing in would have to wait until the appointed day.

Four long months of anticipation leaves a lot of room for people to imagine worst-case scenarios. The people on whose necks Bryan's ax was going to fall had plenty of food for that imagination.

But even the winning side had reasons for doubts. Will this politician, like so many before him, abandon the promises he made to his base now that he gained the power he craved?

We can relate. We have this same question in our own day, don't we? Will the people we send to Washington actually keep the promises they ran on? You never really know until it's too late to do anything about it.

Look at John McCain, for example. War hero or not, after running a campaign to do away with Obamacare he enraged his base by casting the deciding vote to keep Obamacare alive with that infamous thumbs-down.

More recently, Biden ran as a moderate, telling us that he had "defeated the socialists" and that "I am the Democrat Party right now"…only to push such a hard-Left agenda after taking office that he might almost make Bernie Sanders blush.

Trump, on the other hand, enraged Washington for a very different reason. The forty-fifth president had the audacity to follow through on promises like tax reform and relocating the American embassy to Jerusalem. (That last one, for instance, had been promised, but not delivered, by each of the three previous presidents.)

And what about this quirky prophecy that March 4 of this same year will never see a sunrise?

In our real-world timeline, McKinley's inauguration took place on a lovely day with clear skies at noon; it was forty degrees and clear. But the author of this work of fiction was free to use all kinds of metaphors and allusions, including poetic license with the weather.

These literary devices ranged from regular references to passages of scripture and biblical themes which a much more biblically literate culture would have immediately recognized for their original context.

Throughout his work, he casually drops in KJV Bible references like "tax collectors" and "money changers," for example, or phrases like "prophet without honor," expecting his readers to already know them and their context so that he can use them as shorthand. Such references serve to add the weight and meaning of a familiar story to the point he's making without slowing down to explain the ideas those references carry with them.

A secular equivalent might be dropping a casual reference to magic beans or the emperor with no clothes into a story.

But Lockwood also tapped into humanity's perennial interest in the spooky and unexplained, the same vein Edgar Allan

Poe had tapped into many years earlier, or that contemporary (to him, anyway) fiction like *The Picture of Dorian Gray* or *The Turn of the Screw* also tapped into. Brahm Stoker's classic, *Dracula*, would be released the following year.

With what may have been a nod to Shakespeare, chapter 4 included a prophecy that was so absurd on its face that it could not possibly be true...could it? And that was exactly the point.

Inauguration Day came, and the clouds were so heavy overhead that dawn had long since come and gone before the daylight finally peeked through. That "sign" was not enough to dim the spirits of the crowds assembled for that day, but the foreshadowing provides a subtle signal to the reader.

Something is very wrong.

Grand signs in the sky or not, life on Earth continues, and the business of the day went forward without missing a beat. What Bryan did that day set the tone for all that was to follow.

Anyone harboring fears (or hopes?) that Bryan would pull back from his promises and serve as a mainstream establishment politician was quickly disabused of that notion by two announcements. The first was his list of candidates, and the second was the executive order he signed within moments of setting foot in the White House.

One of the hard political lessons the Left knows well, but the Right keeps having to learn again and again is that *personnel is policy*. Reagan learned this the hard way. So did Trump—with the mistake of not installing Republicans with a meaningful commitment to the MAGA agenda, as well as the catastrophic error of failing to clean house of any Obama holdovers right from day one.

Speaking of Obama: a quick look at the players in Obama's administration, not to mention the hard-Left activists nominated by Biden, reminds us of how important it is to have people who are on board with your plan in positions of influence really is to your endgame.

As this is being written, one of the most glaring examples of the personnel-is-policy effect is playing out in the consequences of Soros proxy groups throwing millions of dollars into key AG races in blue strongholds around the country.

If you can get an AG elected who lacks any respect for the rule of law, the rules on the books don't really matter. If your guy cherry-picks who does and does not get charged, the laws are no impediment to even nefarious behavior. One woman in New York literally ran for AG on a promise to target and harass the Trump family…and after becoming AG, Letitia James has made good on that promise.

When Bryan announces his cabinet in the fourth chapter, the author underscores just how important this leadership detail really is. This was a clear signal that the Silver agenda Bryan had run on was a promise he really did intend to keep.

The names listed in Bryan's cabinet are very real figures in American history. His choices would be every bit as dramatic in his day as Democrats appointing Alexandria Ocasio-Cortez as head of the Appropriations Committee, or Ilhan Omar as ambassador to Israel might have been in ours.

Here is the list of his cabinet members. William M Stewart (Nevada), Richard P Bland (Missouri), John P. Altgeld (Illinois), Roger Q. Mills (Texas), Henry George (New York), John Gary Evans (South Carolina), William A. Peffer (Kansas), Lafe Pence

(Colorado); notably absent, but for reasons explained later, was Tillman.

What do we know about these appointees?

Stewart had been a Republican and is remembered for his role in helping pass the 15th Amendment, but between 1892 and 1899, he broke from the Republicans and joined with the Silver Party.

Bland was another candidate who had run in the Democratic presidential primary, was a supporter of bimetallism, and cosponsored a bill obligating the government to regularly purchase a set number of silver dollars and put them into circulation.

Altgeld has been introduced in previous chapters, but one historian summed it up this way: His name is "synonymous with the dawn of the Progressive era."

Mills had been a Confederate officer, Missouri senator, a skilled debater, and a tariffs expert in the Ways and Means Committee.

Henry George was an author and political economist who wrote *Progress and Poverty*. He ran for NY mayor in 1886, affiliated with the Labor Party.

Evans would still have been a young man at this point, enjoying a meteoric rise in his home state of South Carolina. He had already served terms as a representative, as a state senator, and then as governor. Tillman, who had close ties both to Evans and Bryan, had hand-picked Evans for this slot.

Peffer was a populist elected in 1891 by the People's Party to the U.S. senate.

What about Lafayette "Lafe" Pence? He was another Populist.

The loyalists were satisfied with his cabinet choices because they understood that personnel is policy.

But why wasn't Bryan's friend and ally Tillman on the list? Tillman was busy serving as the Democratic Senator of South Carolina. His political interests were being represented; they were just being represented by his proxy, the young protégé, Evans.

What kind of man was Tillman? Among other things, he was a white supremacist who rewrote his state's constitution so that it disenfranchised most black South Carolinians and many poor whites, leading to six decades of white Democrats in power.

And what about the executive order Bryan wrote? The Federal Reserve had not yet been established, so he was operating under different rules than we are now.

The newly minted president leaned on the purchasing power of the government itself to push policy in much the same way that Biden has used it to push COVID policy.

In Biden's case, he insisted all federal employees and those doing business with America lined up with whichever heavy-handed COVID protocols were currently fashionable, whether he had any obvious claims to exerting such authority or not, the fictional president mirrored his modern real-world contemporary by using the federal government to set the pace for how business was to be transacted.

Bryan was somewhat more modest in the scope of his EO than Biden was. He ordered the abandoning of the gold reserve, and the resumption of a gold-and-silver standard to be strictly maintained in all of the government's business transactions. It still paved the way for what was to come.

Wall Street shuddered under the news in terms that might just as easily have described the mood and tone there during any of Wall Street's most famous financial crashes.

Many of them stood to be absolutely ruined by this administration's policies—and they understood that there was no one left who could stop it.

4

CHAPTER

Inauguration: The Dawnless Day

There had been a strange prophecy put forth by someone, and it had made its way into the daily journals, and had been laughingly or seriously commented upon, according to the political tone of the paper, or the passing humor of the writer, that the 4th of March 1897, would never dawn upon the American people.

There was something very curious and uncanny about the prediction, and what actually happened was not qualified to loosen the fearful tension of public anxiety, for the day literally and truly never dawned upon the City of Washington, and well deserves its historical name, the "Dawnless Day."

At six o'clock, the hour of daybreak, such an impenetrable pall of clouds overhung the city that there came no signs of day. The gathering crowds could plainly hear the plaintive cries and lamentations put up in the Negro quarters of the city. Not until nearly nine o'clock did the light cease to "shine in darkness," and the darkness begin to comprehend it.

But although it was a cheerless gray day, even at high noon, its heaviness set no weight upon the spirits of the jubilant tens of thousands which completely filled the city and its public parks and ran over into camps and hastily improvised shelters outside the city limits.

Not until the day previous had the president announces the names of those selected for his cabinet. The South and Far West were fairly beside themselves with joy, for there had been from their standpoint ugly rumors abroad for several days.

It had even been hinted that Bryan had surrendered to the "money changers," and that the selection of his Constitutional advisors would prove him recreant to the glorious cause of popular government, and that the Reign of the Common People would remain but a dream of the "struggling masses."

But these apprehensions were short-lived. The young president stood firm and fast on the platform of the parties which had raised him to his proud eminence. And what better proof of his thorough belief in himself and in his mission could he have given than the following:

Secretary of State—William M. Stewart, of Nevada
Secretary of Treasury—Richard P. Bland, of Missouri
Secretary of War—John P. Altgeld, of Illinois
Attorney General—Roger Q. Mills, of Texas
Postmaster General—Henry George, of New York
Secretary Navy—John Gary Evans, of South Carolina
Secretary Interior—William A. Peffer, of Kansas
Secretary Agriculture—Lafe Pence, of Colorado

The first thing that flashed across the minds of many upon glancing over this list of names was the omission therefrom of Tillman's.

What did it mean? Could the young president have quarreled with his best friend, his most powerful coadjutor?

But the wiser ones only shook their heads and made answer that it was Tillman's hand that filled the blank for Secretary of the Navy, left there by the new ruler after the people's own heart. Evans was but a creation of this great Commoner of the South, an image graven with his hands.

The inaugural address was not a disappointment to those who had come to hear it. It was like the man who delivered it—bold, outspoken, unmistakable in its terms, promising much, impatient of precedent, reckless of result; a double confirmation that this was to be the Reign of the Common People, that much should be unmade, and much made over, and no matter how the rich man might cry out in anger or amazement, the nation must march on to the fulfillment of a higher and nobler mission than the impoverishment and degradation of the millions for the enrichment and elevation of the few.

Scarcely had the young president—his large eyes filled with a strange light, and his smooth, hairless visage radiant as a cloudless sky, his wife's arm twined around his, and their hands linked in those of their children—passed within the lofty portal of the White House, than he threw himself into a chair, and seizing a sheet of official paper penned the following order, and directed its immediate promulgation:

EXECUTIVE MANSION,
WASHINGTON D.C.,

MARCH 4th, 1897

Executive Order No. I.

In order that there may be immediate relief in our terrible financial depression now weighing upon our beloved country, consequent and resulting from the unlawful combination of capitalists and money-lenders both in this republic and in England, and that the ruinous and inevitable progress toward a universal gold standard may be stayed, the president orders and directs the immediate abandonment of the so-called "gold reserve," and that on and after the promulgation of this order, the gold and silver standard of the Constitution be resumed and strictly maintained in all the business transactions of the government.

It was two o'clock in the afternoon when news of this now world-famous executive order was flashed into the great banking centers of the country.

Its effect in Wall Street begs description. On the floor of the stock exchange, men yelled and shrieked like painted savages, and, in their mad struggles, tore and trampled each other.

Many dropped in fainting fits or fell exhausted from their wild and senseless efforts to say what none would listen to. Ashen pallor crept over the faces of some, while the blood threatened to burst the swollen arteries that spread in purple network over the brows of others.

When silence came at last, it was a silence broken by sobs and groans. Some wept, while others stood dumb-stricken as if it was all a bad dream, and they were awaiting the return of their poor distraught sense to set them right again.

Ambulances were hastily summoned, and fainting and exhausted forms were borne through hushed and whispering masses wedged into Wall Street, to be whirled away uptown to their residences, there to come into full possession of their senses only to cry out in their anguish that ruin, black ruin, stared them in the face if this news from Washington should prove true.

Commentary on Chapter 5

With the formalities now out of the way, Bryan turned to the twofold business at hand.

The immediate problem was the crowd of fifty thousand hungry and penniless civilians who had streamed into D.C., confident that the friend of the common man would certainly be replacing all the deadwood in the D.C. bureaucracy with fresh blood.

For some reason, they had convinced themselves (or perhaps had been persuaded by some shyster) that any random guy off the street would be eminently qualified for these wonderful new positions that must certainly be awaiting them once their new president took office.

The long game centered on steps Bryan would need to take in order to move his expansive agenda forward.

He turned his attention first to the people. The president offered them help, but that help did not come in the form of cushy government jobs as they may have hoped.

He did what comes so naturally to Democrats, deploying military resources for civilian use. The secretary of war was directed to establish camps for these "refugees" with rations and blankets being provided until such time as the government could conduct them safely to their various hometowns. The parallels to Joe Biden's reckless open-border policy speak for themselves.

With that issue delegated and squared away, he was now free to turn his full attention to rolling out his political agenda. Oh! What an agenda that would be.

At this point of the story, it consisted mainly of moving forward with his silver policy. It was the very first thing he signed into law. After that came the consolidation of power details like establishing an income tax on the wealthy, putting an end to the filibuster, federalizing banks, and the proposal of adopting several new states (which would further cement the Democrat hold of the Senate just in case any Northern states might begin to waver in their support).

The value of silver was in freefall due, among other factors, to overproduction. So Bryan's bimetallism program was popular among populists who thought it would solve so many of the nation's financial ills. As with many other Democrat solutions, they would soon discover it would only worsen the problem it set out to solve.

Grover Cleveland had just put an end to the Sherman Silver Purchase Act because it was ballooning America's silver reserves while depleting national gold reserves. What the Silver Party wanted to see implemented made the Silver Purchase Act seem jayvee by comparison.

His very first business was to repeal the Coinage Act of 1873, also called the "Crime of 1873." The Coinage Act had moved the U.S. over to a gold standard instead of the previous bimetal standard. In doing so, it omitted silver dollars from among a revised list of standard legal tender, and (critical to the plot of this story) it ended the right of private citizens to bring their silver bullion to the mint where it could be converted into coins of legal tender.

Modern readers may see income tax as familiar and expected. But permanent income tax as we now recognize it was not adopted until ratification of the 16th Amendment in 1913. The radical new tax in this book was modeled on the 1894 precedent. OK, then, what was that precedent?

It called for a 2 percent tax on incomes more than $4,000 a year…in 1894 dollars. That was considered a *big* tax. So…is that more than *you* are paying?

Democrats then, like Democrats today, think the rich aren't paying their share, and need to lighten the load for the poor. They like nebulous ideas like "fair share" rather than concrete numbers and hard percentages that would expose as lies the claim that the "rich people" (a term they refuse to define) aren't paying enough.

Does that even make sense? Not according to TaxPolicyCenter.org. If you break income earnings into five groups (quintiles), the lowest 20 percent of earners paid zero taxes in 2018, the most recent year for which they have numbers. The second quintile paid 3.6 percent of the total tax revenue. The third paid 8.9 percent.

So far, 60 percent of the population is paying 12.5 percent of the total tax burden. The next quintile pays another 17.5 percent, meaning that 80 percent of the population pay only 30 percent of the tax burden. That dreaded 1 percent pay 25.9 percent of the country's total taxes all by themselves.

Oh, and as for that 2 percent tax, the one in the book was based upon, it was a flat tax, not a "progressive" tax.

What else does Bryan do that looks like it could have been copied and pasted straight out of the Biden/Harris/Pelosi/Schumer playbook? Well, that filibuster policy stands out as a big example.

Bryan's Democrats didn't want their agenda slowed down by petty things like debates. They were not interested in any free and fair exchange of ideas where majority and minority would cooperate in cobbling together policy solutions that would be generally acceptable to all.

This was something new to American politics—de facto one-party rule. It invited an arena of bare knuckles and brute force. If you have an unaccountable majority, you can pretty much do whatever you want. Right, or fair, or good are secondary issues.

The Democrats have a very important agenda to roll out. They won the election fair and square and elections will have consequences. (Well, they "probably" won it fair and square. It *was* Illinois that gave Bryan the win, after all, and we all know how that Kennedy/Nixon election played out. But don't ever raise questions about election integrity…that's verboten.)

Now that the new administration had a majority, they have a lot of big plans to implement. With an agenda as big as the one they were planning, there was no time to slow down for unwelcome distractions like "debate." The vision is coming from the top down anyway.

There's nothing left to do but rubber stamp this legislation and move on to the next one. One might even say the government needs to pass the bills in order to find out what's in them.

You can see their spirit of partisan triumphalism plainly in the text from chapter 5: "'We're in the saddle at last,' exclaimed a Southern member, 'and we intend to ride on to victory.'"

Why do Democrats care so much about filibusters, both now and in this book? Simply stated, filibusters are bad news—at least when Democrats are in the majority—precisely because they get in the way of Democrats' naked power grabs. It was true in Lockwood's fiction, and it is true in our modern reality.

At least in the book, they had the decency to be honest about their intentions. These days, they masquerade their cynical power grab as a "civil rights" issue.

Federalizing banks brings us right back to the personnel is policy idea. It is the Left's natural impulse to expand government control into as many areas of a person's life as possible, eroding any natural boundaries between the personal and the political. This includes direct or indirect control of companies.

Some authoritarian governments seize control of private companies entirely, but that's not the only way the game can be played. Other governments are more subtle, wrapping businesses up in so much red tape that even the fact of private ownership becomes a distinction without a difference.

In the modern scenario, Biden has chosen some very... unlikely...nominees for key positions in his administration. One of the more egregious examples was Saule Omarova, his comptroller of the currency nominee.

Omarova was withdrawn after a desire to "end banking as we know it" became public. Maybe the "Order of Lenin" she received from the University of Moscow might have been a tip-off...or maybe the stated desire of seeing oil and gas companies go bankrupt.

While that nominee may have been sidelined, many others, with agendas every bit as corrosive, have sailed through the nomination process, bringing with them their designs to alter the very culture and DNA of the institutions they have been appointed to oversee.

Having finally tasted power, the big-government activists do not want to let it go. If that means rigging the game in their own favor, so be it. Split a reliable blue state into two smaller ones for extra senate seats? Give full state status to blue territories? Turn D.C. into a state? Unconstitutionally federalize elections? How about packing SCOTUS? It's all on the table.

Democrats, throughout our history, have found many creative ways to consolidate power. It's only recently that the rest of the country has started to take serious notice of it and raise objections.

Even in instances when courts order them to comply with, for example, purging old voter rolls, states like California find excuses to leave people who have died or changed address on the list. Is there an innocent explanation for someone doing that? You're welcome to suggest it if you can think of one.

And this brings to the last piece of how they will consolidate their power. There is only so much "fundamental change" that can be accomplished in a typical four-year election cycle, especially when we account for all the recesses and work stoppages.

Just think of how much deeper those structural changes could become if legislators worked long hours and didn't take breaks to go home, see their families, or hear from their constituents. After all, their minds are already made up; it isn't as if hearing from a constituent was likely to change any minds.

And so, in the book anyway, this is exactly what they did. Holidays, constituents, and even family members would have to wait. This project was too big and too important for even the slightest delays.

5

CHAPTER

Full Steam Ahead

By proclamation bearing date the 5th day of March 1897, the president summoned both houses of Congress to convene in extraordinary session "for the consideration of the general welfare of the United States, and to take such action as might seem necessary and expedient to them on certain measures which he should recommend to their consideration, measures of vital import to the welfare and happiness of the people, if not to the very existence of the Union and the continuance of their enjoyment of the liberties achieved by the fathers of the republic."

While awaiting the day set for the coming together of the Congress, the "Great Friend of the Common People" came suddenly face to face with the first serious business of his administration.

Fifty thousand people tramped the streets of Washington without bread or shelter. Many had come in quest of office, lured on by the solemn pronouncement of their candidate that there should be at once a clean sweep of these barnacles of the ship of State and so complete had been their confidence in their glorious young captain, that they had literally failed to provide themselves with either "purse or script or shoes," and now stood hungry and footsore at his gate, begging for a crust of bread.

But most of those making up this vast multitude were "the unarmed warriors of peaceful armies" like the one once led by the redoubtable Coxey, decoyed from farm and hamlet and plantation by some nameless longing to "go forth" to stand in the presence of this new Savior of Society, whose advent to power was to bring them "double pay" for all their toil.

While on the march all had gone well, for their brethren had opened their hearts and their houses as these "unarmed warriors" had marched with flying banners and loud huzzahs though the various towns on the route.

But now the holiday was over, they were far from their homes, and they were in danger of perishing from hunger. What was to be done?

"They are our people," said the president, "their love of country has undone them; the nation must not let them suffer, for they are its hope and its shield in the hour of war, and its glory and its refuge in times of peace. They are the common people for whose benefit this republic was established. The kings of the earth may desert them; I never shall."

The secretary of war was directed to establish camps in the parks and suburbs of the city and to issue rations and blankets to these luckless wanderers until the government could provide for their transportation back to their homes.

On Monday, March 15th, the president received the usual notification from both houses of Congress, that they had organized and were ready for the consideration of such measures as he might choose to recommend for their action.

The first act to pass both houses and receive the signature of the president was an act repealing the Act of 1873 and opening the mints of the United States to the free coinage of silver at the ratio of sixteen to one with gold, and establishing branch mints in the cities of Denver, Omaha, Chicago, Kansas City, Spokane, Los Angeles, Charleston, and Mobile.

The announcement that reparation had thus been made to the people for the "Crime of 1873" was received with loud cheering on the floors and in the galleries of both houses.

And the Great North heard these cheers and trembled.

The next measure of great public import brought before the House was an act to provide additional revenue by levying a tax upon the incomes, substantially on the lines laid down by the legislation of 1894.

The Republican senators strove to make some show of resistance to this measure, but so solid were the administration ranks that they only succeeded in delaying it for a few weeks.

This first skirmish with the enemy, however, brought the president and his followers to realizing a sense that not only must the Senate be shorn of its power to block the "new movement of regeneration and reform" by the adoption of rules cutting off prolonged debate, but that the "new dispensation" must at once proceed to increase its senatorial representation, for who could tell what moment one of the Northern Silver states might not slip away from its allegiance to the "Friend of the Common People."

The introduction of a bill repealing the various civil service acts passed for the alleged purpose of "regulating and improving the civil service of the United States," and of another repealing the various acts establishing national banks, and substituting United States notes for all national bank notes based upon interest-bearing bonds, opened the eyes of the Republican opposition to the fact that the president and his party were possessed of the courage of their convictions, and were determined, come good report or evil report, to wipe all conflicting legislation from the statute books.

The battle in the Senate now took on a spirit of extreme acrimony; scenes not witnessed since the days of slavery were of daily occurrence on the floors of both the House and the Senate.

Threats of secession came open from the North only to be met with the jeers and laughter of the silver and populist members.

"We're in the saddle at last," exclaimed a Southern member, "and we intend to ride on to victory!"

The introduction of bills for the admission of New Mexico and Arizona, and for the division of Texas into two States to be called East Texas and West Texas, although each of these measures was strictly within the letter of the Constitution, fell among the members of the Republican opposition like a torch in a house of tinder.

There was fire at once, and the blaze of party spirit leapt to such dangerous heights that the whole nation looked on in consternation.

Was the Union about to go up in a great conflagration and leave behind it but the ashes and charred pedestals of its greatness?

"We are the people," wrote the president in lines of dignity and calmness. "We are the people and what we do, we do under the holy sanction of law, and there is no one so powerful or so bold as to dare to say we do not do well in lifting off the nation's shoulders the grievous and unlawful burdens which preceding Congresses have placed upon them."

And so the "Long Session" of the Fifty-Fifth Congress was entered upon, fated to last through summer heat and autumn chill and until winter came again and the Constitution itself set limits to its lasting.

And when that day came, and its speaker, amid a wild tumult of cheers arose to declare it ended not by their will, but by the law of the land, he said:

"The glorious revolution is in its brightest bud. Since the president called upon us to convene in last March, we have with the strong blade of public indignation, and with a full sense of our responsibility, erased from the statute books the marks of our country's shame and our people's subjugation.

"Liberty cannot die. There remains much to be done in the way of building up. Let us take heart and push on. On Monday, the regular session of this Congress will begin. We must greet our loved ones from the distance. We have no time to go home and embrace them."

Commentary on Chapter 6

Have you ever noticed that the Left hardly ever defends their ideas by directly and dispassionately comparing them to the pros and cons of rival ideas?

Most of the time, they beeline for the emotional arguments. They present their ideas as the moral imperative, and anything that would oppose them is at best ignorant and at worst, evil. They love a storyline that can be reframed into "victims" and "oppressors," because that gives you a handy shortcut.

Instead of tedious work like closely considering ideas and their implications, you can just attach a "bad" idea to a "bad" person, convince your audience that the bad person is bad, and then his bad idea is automatically discredited with it.

It seldom gets quite as blatant as the following example, but you've almost certainly seen something that is embarrassingly similar to this "logic: "Oh, you're punctual, are you? Do you know who *else* was punctual? Hitler!"

You will notice that the Left never concedes the moral high ground to anyone else. They, and they alone, are always on the "right" side of history. Their policies are—by virtue of being presented by someone on the Left—deeply moral, and heavily salted with words like "justice."

Of course, since their ideas are in conflict with someone else's, it sets up a morality play, a battle between good and evil, rather than a straightforward debate about which solution to a specific problem would produce the best result.

You are not allowed to be neutral. If they are the champions and defenders of truth, their quixotic project isn't complete until it also has a victim worth defending, and a monster worth fighting.

This chapter pulls no punches in both of those categories.

It opened with a Republican doing exactly what politicians have done for as long as politicians have gone to Washington— calling to adjourn proceedings for the usual holiday break.

Not only does such adjournment allow elected officials to return home to their families, but it also lets them hear from the local people whose interests they were called to represent. It lets them mingle among people from their own district so they can see, firsthand, the impact of any policies they have made. It keeps them from living in isolation among a bubble of the Washington insiders.

How did Bryan's party react to that very ordinary act? They ripped it apart with soaring rhetoric of their own importance, and heavy-handed slanders against the villains of society they were morally obligated to make war against.

The Democrats refused to adjourn. There was simply far too much work left to be done. There were far too many American victims that needed immediate rescuing by their saviors in the Democratic Party.

How could any of them, in good conscience, rest with so many victims needing to be rescued?

The "victims" Democrats had in mind then are not so different from the ones they point to now. The "servants of the people" cannot possibly rest with such a task before them.

They paint vivid, emotive pictures of just who needs to be rescued, invoking the "embers of the poor man's hearthstone,"

51

"weeds and thorns" in the fields of the farmers, and "pockets of the laboring man" and "grind the faces of the poor."

Of course, if they are to be rescued, there must be a danger menacing them from which they must be rescued. They have their villains in mind. Naturally, they paint colorful and emotive pictures of them, too.

The villains were coal barons whose feet were on those hearthstones, or railway magnates, or "rapacious landlords," or "enemies of humankind" who were "engaged in drawing their unholy millions from the very life-blood of the nation."

Who could possibly adjourn now, when so desperate a people still awaited their emancipation from their economic overlords? And yes, the Democrats, then as now, really were so brazen and lacking in self-awareness as to invoke the word "emancipation."

Change a few words, and that speech could have just as easily rolled off the lips of Pelosi or Schumer. Update this same speech to 21st century examples of the very *same* words and it might have come off the lips of Bernie Sanders or Rashida Tlaib.

What was their stated endgame? They were setting up a new kind of government that they called the "Reign of the Common People." Pay no attention to the fact that these same common people who had marched to Washington to get a piece of that new system had returned home again, empty-handed, while the Democrats themselves were already consolidating their power.

Instead of adjourning, they pressed on, cranking out more legislation that would remake America in a new image. Their legislation was "calculated to awaken an intense feeling of enthusiasm among the working classes."

In other words, their policy choices were driven by emotional considerations rather than rational ones.

Among other things, there was a Loan Commission, offering zero-interest loans to farmers; there was an act to create a permanent Department of Public Works overseeing work on public buildings, rivers, and harbors.

Yes, Lockwood foresaw the Democrats' love of make-work infrastructure programs coming from a long way off.

Is it any surprise, more than a century later, that so many of the trillions Pelosi wanted to add to the national debt in her profligate spending were creatively rebranded as "infrastructure" programs?

When you keep reading, you see what was listed as "most important of all" of the Bryan Democrats' new programs to help the common man.

The highest priority was the federalizing of railway (e.g., the infrastructure of interstate travel) and the telegraph (e.g., the infrastructure of communications). The government would have final say on fares and schedules, from which there could be no appeal.

Biden ignoring limits on his authority and using federal agencies as an "end run" around Constitutional rights to enforce vaccine mandates or an eviction moratorium that the government has no power to enforce is little more than a natural extension of this same kind of thinking.

So is his administration's open cooperation with Big Tech to crush the First Amendment rights of political dissenters. And that loan commission bears a striking resemblance to government interference that laid the foundation of the financial collapse in 2008.

In the sixth chapter, Bryan's Congress did take one ceremonial vacation day. They made a great show of taking George

Washington's birthday off, to celebrate all the grand achievements of the past year.

Bryan boasted about how his administration had solved all these problems and that the nation was a far better place now that they were in power. Taking those boasts at face value, one might assume they had all but abolished the hardship and suffering we find in everyday life.

Everybody except the Scrooges in big business and banking is thriving and happy...and shouldn't we all thank God that those scoundrels are suffering?

Even the language of a secular day off was imbued with observance for being somehow "sacred."

We don't see the same thing still happening today, do we?

We don't see cherry-picked employment numbers about people returning to work (despite the economy missing jobs targets) as COVID restrictions are finally relaxed and people can return to work, do we? Surely, we didn't see Biden carelessly neglecting to mention that the net buying power of American families fell by 2 percent year over year because of inflation when he was bragging about the average worker getting roughly 5 percent increase in yearly wages.

We couldn't possibly hear overheated rhetoric about how the "sacred" temple of democracy was desecrated on January 6 of 2021.

All sarcasm aside, what about when Democrats were pushing to federalize elections, overstepping boundaries that explicitly define election law as a State responsibility?

Are we supposed to believe it was mere coincidence that Schumer, Pelosi, and Biden invoked MLK Day to push a legislative bill named after civil rights icon John Lewis while insisting that racial minorities are being "repressed" and "denied" the right to vote?

This from the same group of people who are offended when we celebrate Thanksgiving, Columbus Day, or even Independence Day or Memorial Day. There are always some naysayers who will use that "sacred" opportunity to tell us how horrible we are.

The spin doctors in Bryan's world and in ours are happy to report on the world as the Democrat demagogues see it... oblivious to the second-order consequences of the world he has just created.

Bryan's vision in this story is narrow, focused on one thing: of being remembered one day as a hero to the common man.

Joe Biden is a mediocre man with fifty years of public service but little to show for it, beyond the "high-tech lynching" of Justice Clarence Thomas, and being Obama's sidekick. But he dreams of being the next FDR.

If he's letting his party be hijacked by the hard Left after running as a so-called "moderate" who insisted he had "defeated the socialists" in his party, an insecure desire for "legacy" would go a long way to explaining why he's letting it happen.

As we might expect from our own contemporary politicians, even then the swamp was invoking language of "justice" and "oppression" to justify their work of intentionally smashing the foundations upon which our nation was built.

6
CHAPTER

Doubling Down on Early Wins

When a Republican member of the House arose to move the usual adjournment for the holidays, there was a storm of hisses and cries of "no, no!"

Said the leader of the House, amid deafening plaudits: "We are the servants of the people. Our work is not yet complete. There must be no play for us while coal barons stand with their feet on the ashes of the poor man's hearthstone, and weeds and thorns cumber the fields of the farmer for lack of money to buy seed and implements. There must be no play for us while railway magnates press from the pockets of the laboring man six and eight percent return on thrice watered stocks, and rapacious landlords, enriched by inheritance, grind the faces of the poor. There must be no play for us while enemies of the human kind are, by means of trust and combination and 'corners,' engaged in drawing their unholy millions from the very life-blood of the nation, paralyzing its best efforts, and setting the blight of intemperance and indifference upon it, by making life but one long struggle for existence, without a gleam of rest and comfort in old age. No, Mr. Speaker, we must not adjourn, but by our efforts in these halls of legislation let the nation know that we are at work for its emancipation, and by these means let the monopolies and money changers be brought to a realizing sense that the Reign of the Common People has really been entered upon, and then the bells will ring out a happier, gladder New Year than has ever dawned upon this republic."

The opposition fairly quailed before the vigor and earnestness of the "new dispensation" there were soon before the House and pressed well on toward final passage a number of important measures calculated to awaken an intense feeling of enthusiasm among the working classes.

Among these was an act establishing a Loan Commission for the loaning of certain moneys of the United States to farmers and planters without interest; an act for the establishment of a permanent Department of Public Works, its head to be styled secretary of Public Works, rank as a cabinet officer, and supervise the expenditure of all public moneys for the construction of public buildings and the improvement of rivers and harbors; an act making it a felony, punishable with imprisonment for life, for any citizen or combination of citizens to enter into any trust or agreement to stifle, suppress, or in any way interfere with full, open, and fair competition in trade and manufacture among the states, or to make use of any interstate railroads, waterways, or canals for the transportation of any food products or goods, wares, or merchandise which may have been "cornered," stored, or withheld with a view to enhance the value thereof; and most important of all, a preliminary act having for its object the appointment of commissioners for the purchase by the federal government of all interstate railway and telegraph lines, and in the meantime the strict regulation of all fares and charges by a government commission, from whose established schedules there shall be no appeal.

On Washington's birthday, the president issued an Address of Congratulation to the people of the United States, from which the following is extracted:

> The malicious prognostications of our political opponents have proven themselves to be but empty sound and fury. Although not quite one year has elapsed since I, agreeable to your mandate, restored to you the money of the Constitution, yet from every section of our Union comes the glad tidings of renewed activity and prosperity.
>
> The workingman no longer sits cold and hungry beside a cheerless hearthstone; the farmer has taken heart and resumed work; the wheels of the factory are in motion again; the shops and stores of the legitimate dealer and trader are full of bustle and action. There is content everywhere, save in the counting-room of the money changer, for which thank God and the common people of this republic.
>
> The free coinage of that metal which the Creator, in His wisdom, stored with so lavish a hand in the subterranean vaults of our glorious mountain ranges, has proven a rich and manifold blessing for our people. It is in every sense of

the word the "people's money," and already the envious world looks on in amazement that we have shown our ability to do without "foreign cooperation."

The Congress of our republic has been in almost continuous session since I took my oath of office, and the administration members deserve your deepest and most heartfelt gratitude. They are rearing for themselves a monument more lasting than chiseled bronze or polished monolith. They knew no rest, they asked for no respite from their labors until, at my earnest request, they adjourned over to join their fellow citizens in the observance of this sacred anniversary.

Fellow citizens, remember the bonds which a wicked and selfish class of usurers and speculators fastened upon you, and on this anniversary of the birth of the father of our country, let us renew our pledges to undo completely and absolutely their infamous work, and in public assembly and family circle, let us by new vows confirm our love of right and justice, so that the great gain may not slip away from us, but go on increasing so long as the statute books contain a single trace of the record of our enslavement.

As for me, I have but one ambition, and that is to deserve so well of you that when you come

to write my epitaph, you set beneath my name
the single line:

Here lies a friend of the common people.

Commentary on Chapter 7

Passing a law to keep silver at parity with gold did nothing to keep the real value of silver from dropping when the economy was (predictably) flooded with silver coins.

They [the new government] tried to scapegoat Wall Street, but people knew better…and silver's value dropped like a stone.

What was the government's solution? It looked a lot like Build Back Better. Tax the rich and dump more money into the economy through infrastructure projects and handouts.

Silver's value eventually dropped so much that people were carrying it in baskets and carelessly dumping it in piles.

By the time we get to chapter 7, the Bryan administration finds itself in a death spiral of inflation. The only card it has left to play is to double down and hope the situation resolves itself.

This chapter highlights three key ideas.

- Economic laws, like physics, are inviolable.
- Unchecked inflation has nasty consequences.
- Democrats/progressives have a standard response when their policies inevitably fail.

Writing legislation stating that there is a fixed relationship between the value of silver to gold doesn't work. Especially when you suddenly introduce a massive surplus of silver to the equation.

You can artificially prop the value up for a little while, but eventually, reality kicks in and the markets will make their own adjustments without asking anyone's permission to do so. We can't wish away market forces and economic values.

There are real push-and-pull dynamics at work in bringing these prices to a place of equilibrium, and those forces really don't care about what some bureaucrat with an agenda has to say about it.

Even cheating, like artificial price fixing, takes you only so far. What kind of artificial price fixing? The kind that showed up in Bryan's very first act of legislation. It was the one that set in law the exchange rate between silver and gold at a fixed sixteen-to-one ratio pegged to the value of the dollar.

When you inject a massive surplus of silver into that equation, everything else gets thrown out of whack.

With no limiting principle on how much raw silver could be minted into coins by the public (or, in our modern equivalent, printing money so it makes the "money printer go brrr"), currency started losing value. Whenever that happens, money begins losing buying power.

Be careful what you ask for. After years of recession, progressives thought it would be a wonderful thing if inflation eroded the buying power of the dollar. Their hope was that inflation could increase basic income *relative to the value of old debts*, and, in some sense, let the public cheat their way out of indebtedness. (Some on the Left today have the same attitude toward inflating our way out of *federal* debt…without giving any special thought to which citizens could be most hurt by the inflated cost of living.)

When inflation started kicking in, mobs, who had been trained to eat from Uncle Sam's hand, ran to D.C., demanding "justice" from their federal "savior." The government answered their pleas in exactly the way you might expect.

When the dominoes of natural consequences began to fall, Bryan's administration rushed to the rescue with the same two-part plan Democrats so frequently default to: class warfare and big-government solutions.

Wall Street, bankers, and big business were at fault, you see. (Notice hints of Joe Biden's blaming of the meat industry for inflation in his first year?) They must be made to pay their fair share, whatever that is, and to "shoulder the burden" of the taxes which their broad shoulders can surely bear. Tax anything and everything we can to squeeze the rich.

Why would they need to raise taxes? Well, *somebody* would have to pay for their grand promises. Bryan's promises were, indeed, grand.

Naturally, there were pointless make-work infrastructure projects that kept workers busy without regard for actually delivering anything of value for the taxpayer dime. They applied the principles of central planning to farmer's loans, and we saw how well government involvement in loans worked in 2008, didn't we?

They vilified investment instruments as though that, rather than government policy, had created the looming inflation problem. And it wasn't just a little problem. The enormous silver supply told the same sad story of hyperinflation we'd later see in real-world situations like the Weimar Republic, Zimbabwe, or Venezuela, with people carrying money by the wheelbarrow, and individual units of currency being carelessly flung around because they carried almost no value.

If you were to retell this chapter in the modern-day setting, you'd have to imagine every ordinary purchase—a morning cup of coffee, groceries and utilities, taxes, and mortgage payments—being conducted in pennies.

Are they legal tender? Well, sure. But nobody wants to be *paid* in pennies. They're a hassle, and totally unmanageable. People dreaded payday and brought someone along to help carry the weight.

By the end of the chapter, the public hated the very word *silver*.

So what happened to hammer the second year of Bryan's presidency? What changed public opinion so quickly as to turn the once-vaunted "people's dollar" to a word they now hated?

To really understand the role of silver in this story, and what accounted for its rise and fall, we'll first need to look at the political lay of the land in the 1890s. We'll need to wrap our minds around how topics as ridiculously boring as monetary policy and the mint became *the* critical issue of the election of 1896, both in this novel and in the actual historical record.

It is important to remember that this election came in the final months of what was known as the Long Depression in both North America and Europe. Until the 1930s came along, this was the period of time *most* associated with financial hardship at the national level.

So there was an especially broad appeal for any message offering solutions to concerns of the poor, struggling masses.

Next, a historical accident, made because of an oversight in the passing of President Grant's rewriting of coinage policy, stirred passionate debate about who had the right to mint money.

Could the ordinary man melt as much of his silver or gold as he wanted into legal tender? Or did banks have the right to limit the production of currency?

That historical accident was the so-called Crime of 1873 (a term used in Lockwood's book), or the Coinage Act of 1873.

With the use of paper (or digital) money today, *minting* new money by the public is not the concern it once was. But when the government injects boatloads of new money into the economy by printing it, it has the same effect.

This means the question of currency devaluation is every bit as fresh and relevant today as it was when it was raised back in 1896.

If an authentic U.S. coin were made of a certain quality of silver, by weight, should the ordinary citizen be allowed to bring in his ordinary silver to have it melted into ready currency? Or are there sound financial arguments for having the money supply overseen by institutions who would do their best to balance real-world supply and demand to keep the value of money from fluctuating too wildly?

The Democrats explained their monetary policy in their official platform from that year, that document can be found in full in Appendix C.

Some of their key ideas included:

- An insistence that silver be the unit on which the dollar was to be pegged
- Free and unlimited coinage—the right of any citizen to convert raw silver into coins of the same value

- Claims that the gold standard is anti-American and antiliberty
- Establishing a set sixteen-to-one ratio between the value of silver and gold

Both of the major parties had been advocating the gold standard, while a populist party had sprung up calling for bimetallism, and the Populist (Silverite) Party had picked up some elected seats. The support they were getting was from Western mining states which had opened up some rich silver mines, and from farmers who had been suffering from deflation as the recession worsened.

It was a policy clash between the haves and have-nots. Progressive Democrats promised that minting massive quantities of silver was a great way to kick-start a struggling economy. Inflation was one of the intended objectives of that policy, because if the value of the dollar goes up, you can pay off old debts taken out for uninflated dollar amounts and repay them with inflated dollars.

Sure, the banks would get hosed, but that was kind of the point. It was a *feature* of this plan, not a bug. All through this book (just like in modern politics) you will notice that the rich guys are basically the devil incarnate anyway. If they suffer an injustice, they're the bad guys and deserve it; anything that results in their suffering is intrinsically a good thing.

What happened that the Democrats' plan went so horribly, horribly wrong?

Economic laws of supply and demand kicked in. There was a massive oversupply of silver dollars since anyone who wanted to change physical silver into dollar coins was free to do so.

Why else was there a massive oversupply of silver? The mid-19th century produced a series of silver discoveries around the country, and there was an abundance of silver being mined. Supply was up.

A policy allowing the unlimited minting of coins would let silver miners bypass the risk and expense of selling silver on a commodities market in which surplus and scarcity drive the price of the product.

Overabundant silver could be exchanged for dollars at a set rate, no matter how much was produced or how little demand there was for the metal.

Abundance drives down the worth of silver, while the scarcity of gold remains unchanged. Unfortunately for the Americans in this chapter, that drove down the value of the dollar attached to it. Worse still, since the silver-to-gold exchange rate was fixed, a sly investor could get cheap silver, melt it into dollar coins, immediately exchange those silver coins for gold ones, melt down the gold, and sell it by weight. And then… reinvest the profit and do it again.

It's exactly what Gresham's law would have predicted would happen, with "bad money chasing out good money."

Laws of economics do not bend to the will of laws or politicians. An oversupply of currency can and will crash the value of the currency. This is precisely the fear that even Democratic Senator Joe Manchin has been warning Biden's administration about in the modern era.

What happens with an oversupply of currency, whether silver or paper, is the precise mirror image of what we have been seeing with skyrocketing fuel prices since Biden has scrapped the XL Pipeline and placed a mountain of restrictions on the energy sector.

We don't mint more dollar coins like they did in Lockwood's book. No, when we make the same blunders that they did, we are far more sophisticated in how we make them. We do it by firing up our money printers and running them 24/7 or by calling it fancy, official-sounding names like "Modern Monetary Policy."

A cursory search on money printing brought one story from May of 2021 that was already raising alarms about how quickly money was being printed. The headline used stark language: "40% of US Dollars in Existence Were Printed in the Last 12 Months: Is America Repeating the Same Mistake of 1921 Weimar Germany?"[1]

The Weimar Republic is pretty much the textbook case of how inflation can reduce a modern economy to total collapse and the people to desperation.

Absent that economic collapse, and the public unrest, Adolf Hitler might never have risen to his position of power.

In Bryan's America, even the legislation pegging the value of gold to silver broke under the strain of the laws of economics.

This chapter paints a vivid picture of how worthless a devalued currency is, and how powerless even a supposedly well-meaning government is to hit the brakes once the train has begun to derail.

Consequences need to take their natural course as markets correct themselves…however ugly those consequences might be

Meanwhile, in Biden's America, as we make our way through the second year of his administration and approach midterm elections, every instinct we see exhibited across Dem leadership is to double down on every so-called progressive policy.

In the book—as in real life—we will find, as Manchin himself has warned his own party, that this is exactly the wrong reaction to the inflation problem, making it worse and not better.

7

CHAPTER

Inflation: The Bill Always Comes Due

The first year of the silver administration was scarcely rounded up, ere there began to be ugly rumors that the government was no longer able to hold the white metal at a parity with gold.

"It is the work of Wall Street," cried the friends of the president, but wiser heads were shaken in contradiction, for they had watched the sowing of the wind of unreason and knew only too well that the whirl wind of folly must be reaped in due season.

The country had been literally submerged by a silver flood which had poured its argent waves into every nook and cranny of the republic, stimulating human endeavor to most unnatural and harmful vigor.

Mad speculation stalked over the land. People sold what they should have clung to, and bought what they did not need. Manufacturers heaped up goods for which there was no demand, and farmers ploughed where they had not drained, and drained where they were never fated to plough.

The small dealer enlarged his business with more haste than judgment, and the widow drew her mite from the bank of savings to buy land on which she was destined never to set foot.

The spirit of greed and gain lodged in every mind, and the "common people" with a mad eagerness loosened the strings of their leather purses to cast their hard-earned savings into wild schemes of profit. Every scrap and bit of the white metal that they could lay their hands upon, spoons hallowed by the touch of lips long since closed in death, and cups and tankards from which grandsires had drunken were bundled away to the mints to be coined into "people's dollars."

At the very first rumor of the slipping away of this trusted coin from its parity with gold, there was a fearful awakening, like the start and the gasp of the miser who sees his horded treasure melting away from before his eyes, and he not able to reach out and stay its going.

Protest and expostulation first, then came groans and prayers, from which there was an easy road to curses. The working man threw off his cap and apron to rush upon the public square and demand his rights. Mobs ran together, processions formed, deputations hurried off to Washington, not on foot like the Coxey Army, but on the swift wings of the Limited Express.

The "common people" were admitted to the bar of the house, their plaints patiently listened to, and reparation promised. Bills for increased revenue were hurriedly introduced, and new taxes were loaded upon the broad shoulders of the millionaires of the nation—taxes on checks, taxes on certificates of incorporation, taxes on deeds and mortgages, taxes on pleasure yachts, taxes on private parks and pleasances, taxes on wills of all property above $5,000 in value, taxes on all gifts of realty for and in consideration of natural love and affection, taxes on all passage tickets to foreign lands, and double taxes on the estates of all absentees on and after the lapse of six months.

There was a doubling up too of the tariff on all important luxuries, for as was said on the floor of Congress, "if the silks and satins of American looms and the wines and tobacco of native growth, are not good enough for my Lord of Wall Street, let him pay the difference and thank heaven that he can get them at that price."

To quiet the murmurs of the good people of the land, additional millions were placed to the credit of the Department of Public Works, and harbors were dredged out in one month only to fill up in the next, and new systems of improvement of interstate waterways were entered upon on a scale of magnitude hitherto undreamt of.

The commissioners for the distribution of public moneys to farmers so impoverished as to be unable to work their lands, were kept busy in placing "Peffer Loans" where the need of them seemed to be the greatest, and to put a stop to the "nefarious doings of money changers and traders in the misfortunes of the people, a statute was enacted making it a felony punishable with imprisonment for life, for any person or corporate body to buy and sell government bonds or public funds, or deal in them with a view to draw gain or profit from their rise and fall in value.

But try never so hard, the government found itself powerless to check the slow but steady decline in value of the people's dollar.

By midsummer, it had fallen to forty-three cents, and ere the fair Northland had wrapped itself, like a scornful beauty, in its autumn mantle of gold, the fondly trusted coin had sunk to exactly one-third of the value of a standard gold dollar.

People carried baskets in their arms, filled with the now discredited coin, when they went abroad to pay a debt or make purchase of the necessaries of life.

Huge sacks of the white metal were flung at the door of the mortgagee when discharge was sought for a few thousand dollars.

Men servants accompanied their mistresses upon shopping tours to carry the necessary funds, and leather pockets took the place of the old-time muslin ones in male habiliments, least the weight of the fifteen coins required to make up a five-dollar gold piece should tear the thin stuff and spill a dollar at every step.

All day long in the large cities, huge trucks loaded with sacks of the coin rolled and rumbled over the pavement in the adjustment of the business balances of the day.

The tradesman who called for his bill was met at the door with a coal scuttle or a nail keg filled with the needful amount, and on payday, the working man took his eldest boy with him to "tote the stuff home" while he carried the usual bundle of firewood.

And strange to say, this dollar, once so beloved by the "common people," parted with its very nature of riches and lay in heaps unnoticed and unheeded on shelf or table, until occasion arose to pay it out which was done with a careless and contemptuous toss as if it were the iron money of the ancient Spartans, and Holy Writ for once at least, was disproven and discredited for the thief showed not the slightest inclination to "break in and steal" where these treasures had been laid up on earth, although the discs of white metal might lie in full view on the table, like so many pewter platters or pieces of tinware.

Men let debts run, rather than call for them, and barter and exchange came into vogue again, the good housewife calling on her neighbor for a loan of flour or meal, promising to return the same in sugar or dried fruit whenever the need might arise.

And still the once magic discs of silver slipped slowly and silently downward, and ever downward in value and good name, until it almost seemed as if the people hated the very name of silver.

Commentary on Chapter 8

With inflation driving an unraveling of the economy, other crises were sure to follow.

Inflation had scared away investors, with the predictable downstream effects on employment and desperation.

With the economy in freefall, people looked for answers among a whole range of political factions. Society began to crack and fragment under the strain, with everyone looking for somewhere to lay the blame.

Labor became hungry, loud, and defiant. Membership rolls of socialists and anarchists swelled. Hard-edged words gave way to open violence. The nation was beginning to tear itself apart.

There were no easy answers to be found.

Suddenly, a well-intentioned president who had once imagined himself to be a great savior of the common man found himself presiding over a runaway train with nothing left to do but hope it would come to a stop without derailing.

Bryan learned, too late, that the forces he had empowered were not actually his own to control. Having already used the president's charisma and skilled oratory to seize unfettered power, others would march forward with agendas of their own, with or without Bryan's consent.

That legacy, that epitaph he had dreamed of someday having, was coming to pieces before his very eyes. Now his thoughts turned not to a faraway legacy, but the more immediate concerns of whether or not he could even make it to the end of his presidency without the country ripping itself to pieces.

What is the truly sobering part of this story? It is this: like so many others who have pushed catastrophic policies at home and abroad, a decent man can support a bad idea.

All evidence suggests the real-world William Jennings Bryan was a genuinely nice and well-meaning guy. His real-world tombstone honors his memory with the words: "Statesman, yet friend to truth. Of soul sincere, in action faithful, and in honor clear."

In some of his last days on the planet, he had participated as part of the prosecution of the now-famous Scopes trial, in which his reputation as a devout man was so unchallenged that it was used by the other side's legal team to their own advantage.

They called him as a witness and expert on Christian scripture. While intended as a sneaky trick, it was still an open appeal to what was perceived of the man's integrity. He was, after all, a ruling elder in the Presbyterian Church.

It is worth pointing out that this chapter leaves room for Bryan's personal integrity and intentions to have remained rooted in goodwill, no matter how catastrophic the actual application of his policy may have been. It is also worth remembering that the same can be true of individuals duped by supposed goodness of "progressive" or "woke" policies today.

How many persuadable people out there may simply have taken the wrong measure of the problem, and remain committed to solutions that are doomed to failure? This is why our system was built on debate and the clash of ideas in civil conversation rather than on conflict and the destruction of people who stand in the way of our objectives.

Some of the more serious problems staring him in the face were the works of his own hand. Not just the economy, but the deepening political strife as well.

When he tried to pull the reins back on the agenda, there was open conflict between him and his party. The president lamented, "I stand alone. The spirits I have called up are no longer obedient to me. My country, my country, how willingly I would give my life for thee if by such a sacrifice I could restore thee to thy old-time prosperity."

It was only then that Bryan first recognized the divisive nature of the "revolutionary propaganda" his party had been leaning into this entire time. There's a lesson there for the rest of us.

What came next was not the jostling of competing visions of how to rightly govern for the good of the nation. What came next was a cut-throat regional partisanship where new power was being used to settle scores and punish regional and political rivals over old grudges.

In the context of Lockwood's book, Democrats in the South— because of their allegiance with Northern Silver states—had been lifted to positions of power. This opened the opportunity to settle scores with the Republicans in the North over how the Civil War had been resolved.

Two regional issues in particular were offensive to the South. Punitive taxes that had been attached to tobacco crops and Confederate widows not being cared for from federal coffers in the same manner as their Union counterparts.

It takes no great imagination to know why the North would be upset about giving money to the soldiers (or their widows) wounded *while fighting for the rebel army.*

But every election has its consequences, right? Not every politician is a statesman committed to governing in a way that's fair to citizens and states in both parties. The South had been waiting for a chance to poke Republicans in the eye, and they were *not* going to waste this opportunity.

How fortunate we are that no such dynamics are at play in modern America, where Congress and Senate can be split with knife's-edge closeness and hardly a thought given to pressing a ruthless partisan agenda.

To listen to the media reporting on events on the Hill, you might almost think that was the case. When one Republican sides with all of the Democrats, that's held up as proof of "bipartisanship."

When legislation passes with straight-line party votes, that's not a dirty, partisan trick. Oh, no. That's the canny use of political power.

But let one or two Democrats side with Republicans, and that's dangerously obstructionist! Whenever Democrats get the short end of that stick, you can be certain that accusations of "dark money" will not lag far behind.

The political flashpoints of more than a century ago may seem distant and insignificant in today's context, but in his day, they were putting direct pressure on an exposed nerve, and they knew it.

It was a classic red state/blue state battle for cultural control. The closest obvious comparison would be the superheated rhetoric on both sides of *Roe v. Wade*. Lesser examples might include divisions over Critical Race Theory (although that has been heating up); immigration; or pitting ecopolicies in direct opposition to the energy sector.

But even the political rancor of the abortion debate can't touch the same deep emotions this flashpoint would draw on with respect to the Civil War.

Taxpayers were being asked to fund the war effort of men who took up arms against the nation: rebels who sent many of their own fathers and brothers to early graves to quell what they saw as government overreach.

Imagine the horror dawning upon the Republicans in that moment when the Democrats from the South made it clear that they would be using their majority to pass the most deeply partisan and objectionable laws the North could imagine...and there was nothing they could do about it.

Someone cried out treason, but could they really be sure? What if this was just a loud and defiant speech, and cooler heads would prevail in the morning? Can a nation already on the knife's edge afford an overreaction to a flash of angry rhetoric?

Some in the North got skittish and began initiating preparations necessary for putting down a second rebellion, should that be required.

But after the initial treasonous outburst, nothing seemed to come of it. Tensions eased just a little and life carried on as it had before.

8

CHAPTER

The Inevitable Crash

The "Fateful year of '99" upon its coming in, found the Republic of Washington in dire and dangerous straits.

The commercial and industrial boom had spent its force, and now the frightful evils of a debased currency, coupled with demoralizing effects of rampant paternalism, were gradually strangling the land to death.

Capital, ever timid and distrustful in such times, hid itself in safe deposit vaults, or fled to Europe.

Labor, although really hard-pressed and lacking the very necessities of life, was loud-mouthed and defiant.

Socialism and anarchism found willing ears into which to pour their burning words of hatred and malevolence, and the consequence was that serious rioting broke out in the larger cities of the North, often taxing the capacities of the local authorities to the utmost.

It was bruited abroad that violent dissensions had arisen in the cabinet, the young president giving signs of a marked change of mind, and like many a man who has appealed to the darker passions of the human heart, he seemed almost ready to exclaim:

"I stand alone. The spirits I have called up are no longer obedient to me. My country, oh, my country, how willingly would I give my life for thee, if by such a sacrifice I could restore thee to thy old-time prosperity."

For the first he began to realize what an intense spirit of sectionalism had entered into this "revolutionary propaganda." He spoke of his fears to none save to his wise and prudent helpmate.

"I trust you, beloved," she whispered, as she pressed the broad, strong hands that held her clasped.

"Aye, dear one, but does my country?" came in almost a groan from the lips of the youthful ruler.

Most evident was it, that thus far the South had been the great gainer in this struggle for power.

She had increased her strength in the Senate by six votes; she had regained her old-time prestige in the House; one of her most trusted sons was in the Speaker's chair, while another brilliant Southron led the administration forces on the floor.

Born as she was for the brilliant exercise of intellectual vigor, the South was of that strain of blood which knows how to wear the kingly graces of power so as best to impress the "common people."

Many of the men of the North had been charmed and fascinated by this natural pomp and inborn demeanor of greatness and had yielded to it.

Not a month had gone by that this now-dominant section had not made some new demand upon the country at large.

Early in the session, at its request, the internal revenue tax, which had rested so long upon the tobacco crop of the South and poured so many millions of revenue into the national treasury, was wiped from the statute books with but a feeble protest from the North.

But now the country was thrown into a state bordering upon frenzy by a new demand, which, although couched in calm and decorous terms, nay, almost in the guise of a petition for long-delayed justice to hard-pressed and suffering brethren, had about it a suppressed, yet unmistakable tone of conscious power and imperiousness which well became the leader who spoke for "that glorious Southland to which this Union owes so much of its greatness and its prestige."

Said he:

> Mr. Speaker, for nearly thirty years our people, although left impoverished by the conflict of the states, have given of their substance to salve the wounds and make green the old age of the men who conquered us.
>
> We have paid this heavy tax, this fearful blood money unmurmuringly. You have for given us for our bold strike for liberty that God willed should not succeed. You have given us back our rights, opened the doors of these sacred halls to us, called us your brothers, but unlike noble Germany who was content to exact a lump sum from "la belle France," and then bid her go in peace and freedom from all further exactions, you have for nearly thirty years laid this

humiliating war tax upon us, and thus forced us year in and year out to kiss the very hand that smote us.

Are we human that we now cry out against it? Are we men that we feel no tingle in our veins after these long years of punishment for no greater crime than that we loved liberty better than the bonds of a confederation laid upon us by our fathers?

We appeal to you as our brothers and our countrymen. Lift this infamous tax from our land, than which your great North is ten thousand times richer.

Do one of two things: Either take our aged and decrepit soldiers by the hand and bless their last days with pensions from the treasury of our common country, for they were only wrong in that their cause failed or remove this hated tax and make such restitution of this blood money as shall seem just and equitable to your soberer and better judgment.

To say that this speech, of which the foregoing is but a brief extract, threw both houses of Congress into most violent disorder, but faintly describes its effect.

Cries of "Treason! Treason!" went up; blows were exchanged and hand-to-hand struggles took place in the galleries, followed by the flash of the dread bowie and the crack of the ready pistol.

The republic was shaken to its very foundations. Throughout the North there was but a repetition of the scenes that followed the firing upon Sumter.

Public meetings were held, and resolutions passed calling upon the government to concentrate troops in and about Washington and prepare for the suppression of a second rebellion.

But gradually this outbreak of popular indignation lost some of its strength and virulence, for it was easy to comprehend that nothing would be gained at this stage of the matter by meeting a violent and unlawful demand with violence and unwise counsels.

Besides, what was it any way but the idle threat of a certain clique of unscrupulous politicians?

The republic stood upon too firm a foundation to be shaken by mere appeals to the passions of the hour. To commit treason against our country called for an overt act. What had it to dread from the mere oratorical flash of a passing storm of feeling?

It is hard to say what the young president thought of these scenes in Congress. So pale had he grown of late that a little more of pallor would pass unnoted, but those who were wont to look upon his face in these troublous times report that in the short space of a few days the lines in his countenance deepened perceptibly, and that a firmer and stronger expression of will-power lurked in the corners of his wide mouth, overhung his square and massive chin, and accentuated the vibrations of his wide-opened nostrils.

He was under a terrible strain. When he had caught up the scepter of power, it seemed a mere bauble in his strong grasp, but now it had grown strangely heavy, and there was a mysterious pricking at his brow, as if that crown of thorns which he had not willed should be set upon the heads of others, were being pressed down with cruel hands upon his own.

Commentary on Chapter 9

What makes countries founded on democratic principles supple and enduring? Many times, they are able to withstand massive social upheavals that topple governments in other systems.

Other countries, with more rigid top-down structures, are vulnerable to different hazards than a democratized nation might be. Monarchs and empires, for example, will have occasional palace intrigues and leadership challenges from would-be heirs to the throne.

Other autocrats or states with single-party rule will have agitators from a political faction foment a revolution. Sometimes, an autocrat just pushes his power too far and the people lose patience and throw him down from his ivory tower.

Democratized countries, on the other hand, have come up with a different way to resolve those problems. They don't rely on mere hope or chance that the citizens won't become so upset that they would take up arms against their leaders. They have developed a system to harness the public's feedback, using that energy to periodically course-correct and keep the system itself running smoothly.

Instead of periods of peace punctuated by violent upheaval and revolution, they have installed an innovative safety valve to give the people a voice, by incorporating a regularly scheduled revolution where the weapon of choice is ballots, not bullets.

But that system has hazards of its own, as our generation knows all too well. That system operates entirely on trust.

The voting public needs to be confident that its voice will be truly heard. Its members need to know that in any given election, a candidate from any party stands a fair shot at winning with nobody rigging the game.

It's the same reason we establish important brakes on the legislative process that give voice to the dissenting loyal minority. Tools like the filibuster, for instance, or the rights of the minority to have their say in who sits on a committee.

The willful trampling of those norms were enormous red flags in the first attempt to impeach Trump as well as Pelosi's heavy-handed refusal of the Republican minority leader to choose his own appointees to the January 6 Committee, hand-picking two Republicans who had voted to impeach Trump for "inciting an insurrection" to lead a supposedly impartial investigation into the events of January 6, 2021.

And that's without yet knowing the full extent of what the Durham report will dig up, even if what it has uncovered so far points us in the worse-than-Watergate direction.

When the public loses faith in the process, the democratic safety valve can no longer serve its purpose correctly.

As citizens in chapter 9 see the "fundamental transformation" taking place in their country, they start to grapple with some of the same questions that have resurfaced in the 21st century—can the red and blue states coexist, or will the time come for a national divorce?

What are the concerns Lockwood puts in the mouths of his fictional contemporaries? The chapter's second paragraph is crammed with them.

Have Dems seized permanent control? Has the agenda of their (socialist) revolution succeeded? Have they loaded the courts and federal government with partisans? Is there a contempt for red-state voters? Are they taxing wealth to oblivion so that they can harness it for any number of unspecified redistribution schemes? Has the Left succeeded in misusing the tools of the republic in the service of capturing America and subjugating anyone who opposes them?

What recourse do you have when you believe the system is failing you?

You are left with few options. You can surrender. You can flee. Or you can continue the fight. Fleeing a bad state for a better one might work if there was a better state to which you could flee. But that would take a commitment to federalism…something not on the menu with Bryan's Dems (and ours, too) frantically federalizing everything.

Surrender? Do you really think the North was willing to surrender to an agenda from the same states whose rebellion their fathers and grandfathers had put down in the Civil War? That's even more unlikely than expecting the children and grandchildren of those who held the line during the Cold War to roll over for a communist agenda.

No, they can't surrender. They can't flee.

The fight must go on. But how? The conventional ways of fighting look like dead ends. There is no opposition in Congress. The presidency is no help. The courts are being packed with loyalists to the socialist cause—businesses are being bum-rushed into bankruptcy and the very nature of the country is being fundamentally transformed by aggressive rewriting of policy by activists who want to turn America into something it's not.

The question being asked is critical.

Can America survive to the end of such a destructive president's term? Can a future election undo the harm being inflicted now, or is it necessary to take more drastic action?

It's a question that has been asked in the context of a "national divorce" today, and it's a question Lockwood grappled with more than a century ago.

What was the drastic "Plan B" solution proposed in the book?

With the drastic cultural differences between the South, the East and the West, the author imagined the strain of the Bryan government putting enough pressure on the natural fault lines of the day that they split apart from a single nation composed of equal states into some new arrangement of three separate entities joined together only for shared federal responsibilities such as national defense.

But even if such a national divorce, or Declaration of Dissolution, was the way forward, how could they make it happen? The new Congress was seated, with even greater populist and socialist sympathies than before, and "no reverence for the old order of things."

How does someone make themselves heard when the government has made it clear it has no intention of listening?

The same way disempowered people have made themselves heard for generations. It's how the Reverend Doctor Martin Luther King Jr. made his voice heard, how Gandhi made his voice heard, and how the truckers in Canada made their voices heard in opposition to tyrannical government.

Show up in large numbers, and your cause may be too big to ignore.

9
CHAPTER

The Nuclear Option

When the last embers of the great conflagration of the rebellion had been smothered out with tears for the lost cause, a prophecy had gone up that the mighty North, rich with a hundred great cities, and strong in the conscious power of its wide empire, would be the next to raise the standard of rebellion against the federal government.

But that prophet was without honor in his own land, and none had paid heed to his seemingly wild words.

Yet now, this same mighty North sat there in her grief and anxiety, with her face turned Southward, and her ear strained to catch the whispers that were in the air. Had not the scepter of power passed from her hand forever? Was not the revolution complete?

Were not the populists and their allies firmly seated in the halls of Congress? Had not the Supreme Court been rendered powerless for good by packing it with the most uncompromising adherents of the new political faith?

Had not the very nature of the federal government undergone a change: Was not paternalism rampant? Was not socialism on the increase? Were there not everywhere evidences of an intense hatred of the North and a firm determination to throw the whole burden of taxation upon the shoulders of the rich man, in order that the surplus revenues of the government might be distributed among those who constitute the "common people?"

How could this section of the Union ever hope to make head against the South, united, as it now was, with the rapidly growing States of the Northwest? Could the magnificent cities of the

North content themselves to march at the tail of Tillman's and Peffer's chariots?

Had not the South a firm hold of the Senate? Where was there a ray of hope that the North could ever again regain its lost power, and could it for a single moment think of entrusting its vast interests to the hands of a people differing with them on every important question of statecraft, pledged to a policy that could not be otherwise than ruinous to the welfare of the grand commonwealths of the Middle and Eastern sections of the Union and their sister states this side of the Mississippi?

It was madness to think of it. The plunge must be taken, the declaration must be made. There was no other alternative, save abject submission to the chieftains of the new dispensation, and the complete transformation of that vast social and political system vaguely called the North.

But this revolution within a revolution would be a bloodless one, for there could be no thought of coercion, no serious notion of checking such a mighty movement. It would be in reality the true republic purging itself of a dangerous malady, sloughing off a diseased and gangrened member—no more, no less.

Already this mighty movement of withdrawals from the Witenagemote [any assembly, parliament, or discursive gathering] of the Union was in the air.

People spoke of it in a whisper, or with bated breath; but as they turned it over and over in their minds, it took on shape and form and force, till at last it burst into life and action like Minerva from Jupiter's brain—full-fledged, full-armed, full-voiced, and full-hearted.

Really, why would it not be all for the best that this mighty empire, rapidly growing so vast and unwieldy as to be only with the greatest difficulty governable from a single center, should be split into three parts, Eastern, Southern and Western, now that it may be done without dangerous jar or friction?

The three republics could be federated for purposes offensive and defensive, and until these great and radical changes could be brought about there would be no great difficulty in devising "living terms," for immediately upon the Declaration of Dissolution, each state would become repossessed of the sovereign powers which it had delegated to the federal government.

Meanwhile the "Fateful year '99" went onward toward its close. The whole land seemed stricken with paralysis, so far as the various industries were concerned, but, as it is wont to be in such times, men's minds were supernaturally active.

The days were passed in the reading of public prints, or in passing in review the weighty events of the hour.

The North was only waiting for an opportunity to act. But the question that perplexed the wisest heads was: How and when shall the Declaration of Dissolution be made, and how soon thereafter shall the North and the States in sympathy with her withdraw from the Union, and declare to the world their intention to set up a republic of their own, with the mighty metropolis of New York as its social, political, and commercial center and capital?

As it came to pass, the North had not long to wait.

The Fifty-Sixth Congress soon to convene in regular session in the city of Washington, was even more populistic and socialistic than its famous predecessor, which had wrought such wonderful changes in the law of the land, showing no respect for precedent, no reverence for the old order of things.

Hence all eyes were fixed upon the capital of the nation, all roads were untrodden, save those which led to Washington.

A Note on Chapter 10

Now for a few considerations before we turn to Lockwood's final chapter.

We remind our readers of the context in which this book was first penned.

It was written in response to issues concerning the 1896 election. That happened to be the year that the Supreme Court made one of its most infamous rulings: *Plessy v. Ferguson*.

With that historical backdrop, we obviously cannot assume that descriptions of racial minorities and their role in society—even literary descriptions—will hold up in the light of modern moral sensibilities.

But for the purpose of this book, they can still serve as a helpful reference point to how different interest groups (political voting blocks, one might say) could have been expected to react to political events if they had played out as the author imagined.

Such a historical characterization is further complicated by the tragic fact that so many black Americans in Lockwood's day would have been denied the opportunity to receive anything resembling a quality education.

Commentary on Chapter 10

The final chapter's opening paragraphs quietly insert an almost throwaway line eerily similar to events we saw in early January of 2021.

Federal troops had been quietly withdrawn from the Capitol. By whose order had they been removed? By the Congress that was quite intent on pressing its agenda forward with, or without, presidential approval. What was the reason those troops were withdrawn? Lockwood explains that, too. "Lest the president [Bryan], in a moment of weakness, do or suffer to be done some act unfriendly to the Reign of the Common People."

This is the rationale by which Constitutional arsonists justified their gutting of America and rebuilding it according to their own agenda. They weren't serving their own agenda, heaven forfend. They merely served the will of the common person. The underserved. The oppressed.

They served the same downtrodden citizens who were, even now, rioting because of the ruinous effects of the policies this unrelenting administration had already enacted in their name.

The match setting off the events that followed was struck when Democrats leveraged their majority to help their states at the expense of, and to the great objection of, Republican states who had no means by which to oppose them.

Not only were they intending to use federal funds (*federal funds!*) to pay the benefits of Confederate soldiers and their widows, but all the war reparations that had been paid by the rebel states would be returned to the states that had paid them.

The act passed through the Senate with little fanfare. But the public took notice, and it responded in force.

Citizens, from North and South alike, streamed into the nation's capital, waiting to see what would happen next, and to urge their respective politicians to vote with or against the bill.

The Fifty-Sixth Congress convened in January of 1899 and things are coming to a boil as this bill remains before the House in late December. There are few if any tricks left to be played by the minority. Even the delaying tactic of the filibuster has been taken from them.

But the Fifty-Sixth Congress is in a hurry to get things done. There is too much on the line, they don't have time to slow themselves down and be held to account by trivialities like precedent or House rules. Adam Schiff and Jerry Nadler would have loved these guys.

The public thronged the streets, knowing something big was going to happen, but not sure what that might be. Women and children could scarcely be seen, but the men were there, sleeping in their clothes when they slept at all, so that they might be ready when the announcement came.

The bill came up for a vote on Saturday, December 30, 1899. But there was so much yelling, and so many disruptions that no progress was made on its passing. Midnight was approaching, and a decision had not yet been made.

Delaying the vote until Monday might cost the Democrats their momentum. Some might lose their nerve and the party solidarity to force the vote might be lost.

If you wonder what that desperation might look like, just remember how the Democrats and their media surrogates raged at Joe Manchin over their failure to pass Joe Biden's Build Back Better agenda, and his refusal to change filibuster rules so they could do an end run around what is explicitly stated within the Constitution and federalize the vote.

What did these zealots do? They did something readers would have been scandalized by in the 1890s and suspended the rules so that Congress would remain in deliberation on a Sunday. The congressmen remained at their seats overnight and into the next day like soldiers expecting an ambush.

Christ himself was misquoted in an effort to justify the setting aside of the day of worship for the service of political wrangling with His teaching on the proper view of the Sabbath.

Even the religious belief of both parties, who occasionally lapsed into singing hymns to mark the fact that it was Sunday, was deeply divided in both style and content.

Factions loyal to the South, whether elected or in the gallery, drew from their Methodist traditions. In the context of a bill that would inflame all the old grievances of the Civil War, it should surprise nobody that the North would reply with "The Battle Hymn of the Republic," or "John Brown's Body."

Day drew into night, and around eleven p.m., the GOP was at the point of exhaustion, unable to continue the fight much longer. Not only were these people all an hour away from midnight and a new day, but of a new year, and even a new century, and all were aware of the knife's edge the republic was walking.

The leader of the minority, at the end of his strength, admits they had used every tool in the toolbelt, to no avail. They could obstruct the vote—and whatever consequences came with it—no longer.

Just when Democrats were about to declare victory and call the vote, a figure appeared at the door. That figure was President Bryan himself.

When the commotion caused by his arrival had subsided, he raised his voice to speak to the crowd. And with a sharp *crack*, he was gaveled out of order.

Here began the familiar dance of invoking competing rules of procedure or order as the executive and legislative pressed their respective authorities as equal branches of government.

The president would speak. The Speaker would object. The president would invoke a privilege, the Speaker would limit the boundaries of that speech, around and around they would go, no different than how we see arcane rules whipped out to advantage one group against the other in the modern day.

The president had invoked his right to address a joint session of Congress on the State of the Union.

When everyone had filed in, there wasn't much left of Bryan. The heartbreak of seeing where his grand vision led his beloved country had taken a toll on him and this was his last, best chance to save it from certain disaster.

As he raised his hand to speak, the bells began to toll midnight. The end of the day, the year, the century, and the beginning of…

That's when the dynamite blew the dome off of the Capitol building. The president never had his chance to make that final speech. Security led him to safety, the senators filed out, and the Speaker took that moment to pass the bill.

Whatever it might be that America would wake up to that gray Monday morning at the dawning of a new century, it was not the same nation Americans knew when they had gone to bed the night before.

10

The Final Gavel

Again, Congress had refused to adjourn over for the holidays.

The leaders of the administration forces were unwilling to close their eyes, even for needful sleep, and went about pale and haggard, startled at every word and gesture of the opposition, like true conspirators, as they were, for the federal troops had been almost to a man quietly removed from the capital and its vicinage, lest the president in a moment of weakness, might do or suffer to be done some act unfriendly to the Reign of the Common People.

Strange as it may seem, there had been very little note taken by the country at large of the introduction at the opening of the session of an act to extend the pension system of the United States to the soldiers of the Confederate armies, and for covering back into the various treasuries of certain States of the Union, such portions of internal revenue taxes collected since the readmission of said states to the federal Congress, as may be determined by commissioners duly appointed under said act.

Was it the calm of despair, the stolidity of desperation, or the cool and restrained energy of a noble and refined courage?

The introduction of the act, however, had one effect; it set in motion toward the national capital, mighty streams of humanity—not of wild-eyed fanatics or unshaven and unkempt politicasters and bezonians—but of soberly clad citizens with a businesslike air about them, evidently men who knew how to earn more than enough for a living, men who paid their taxes and had a right to take a look at the public servants, if desire so moved them.

But very plain was it that the mightier stream flowed in from the South, and those who remembered the capital in antebellum days, smiled at the old familiar sight, the clean-shaven faces, the long hair thrown carelessly back under the broad brim felts, the half unbuttoned waistcoats and turned-down collars, the small feet and neatly fitting boots, the springy loping pace, the soft intonation, the long fragrant cheroot.

It was easy to pick out the man from the Northland, well-clad and well-groomed, as careful of his linen as a woman, prim and trim, disdainful of the picturesque felts, ever crowned with the ceremonious derby, the man of affairs, taking a businesslike view of life, but wearing for the nonce a worried look and drawing ever and anon a deep breath.

The black man, ever at the heels of his white brother, set to rule over him by an inscrutable decree of nature, came forth too in thousands, chatting and laughing gayly, careless of the why or wherefore of his white brother's deep concern, and powerless to comprehend it had he so desired.

Every hour now added to the throng. The broad avenues were none too broad. The excitement increased. Men talked louder and louder; women and children disappeared almost completely from the streets.

The "Southern element" drew more and more apart in knots and groups by itself. Men threw themselves upon their beds to catch a few hours of sleep, but without undressing, as if they were expecting the happening of some portentous event at any moment, the event of their lives, and dreaded the thought of being a moment late.

If all went well, the bill would come up for final passage on Saturday, the thirtieth day of the month, but so fierce was the battle raged against it, and so frequent the interruptions by the contumacy both of members and of the various cliques crowding the galleries to suffocation, that little or no progress could be made.

The leaders of the administration forces saw midnight drawing near with no prospect of attaining their object before the coming in of Sunday on which the House had never been known to sit. An adjournment over to Monday of the New Year might be fatal, for who could tell what unforeseen force might not break up their solid ranks and throw them into confusion.

They must rise equal to the occasion. A motion was made to suspend the rules, and to remain in continuous session until the business before the House was completed. Cries of "Unprecedented!" "Revolutionary!" "Monstrous!" came from the opposition, but all to no purpose; the House settled down to its work with such a grim determination to conquer that the Republican minority fairly quailed before it. Food and drink were brought to the members in their seats; they ate, drank, and slept at their posts, like soldiers determined not to be ambushed or stampeded.

It was a strange sight, and yet an impressive one withal—a great party struggling for long deferred rights—freemen jealous of their liberties, bound together with the steel hooks of determination that only death might break asunder.

Sunday came in at last, and still the struggle went on. "The people know no days when their liberties are at stake," cried the leader of the House. "The Sabbath was made for man and not man for the Sabbath."

Many of the speeches delivered on that famous Sunday sounded more like the lamentations of a

Jeremiah, the earnest and burning utterances of a Paul, or the scholarly and well-rounded periods of an Apollos.

The weary hours were lightened by the singing of hymns by the Southern members, most of them good Methodists, in which their friends and sympathizers in the galleries joined full-throated and fuller-hearted; while at times, clear, resonant and in perfect unison, the voices of the staunch men of the North broke in and drowned out the religious song with the majestic and soul-stirring measures of "John Brown's Body," "Glory, Glory Halleluiah" of which seemed to hush the tumult of the chamber like a weird chant of some invisible chorus breaking in upon the fierce rioting of a Belshazzar's feast.

Somewhat after eleven o'clock, an ominous silence sank upon the opposing camps, the Republican leaders could be seen conferring together nervously.

It was a sacred hour of night, thrice sacred for the great republic. Not only a new year, but a new century was about to break upon the world. A strange hush crept over the turbulent House, and it's still more turbulent galleries.

The Republican leader rose to his feet. His voice sounded cold and hollow. Strong men shivered as they listened.

"Mr. Speaker: We have done our duty to our country; we have nothing more to say, no more blows to strike. We cannot stand here with in the sacred precincts of this Chamber and see our rights as freemen trampled beneath the feet of the majority.

"To have striven to prevent the downfall of the republic, like men sworn to battle against wrong and tyranny, but there comes a time when blank despair seizes upon the hearts of those who struggle against overwhelming odds. That hour has sounded for us. We believe our people, the great and generous people of the North, will cry unto us: 'Well done, good and faithful servants.'

"If we do wrong, let them condemn us. We, every man of us, Mr. Speaker, have but this moment sworn not to stand within this Chamber and witness the passage of this act. Therefore we go…"

"Not so, my countrymen," cried a clear, metallic, far-reaching voice that sounded through the Chamber with an almost supernatural ring in it. In an instant, every head was turned, and a thousand voices burst out with suppressed force: "The president! The president!"

In truth, it was he, standing at the bar of the House, wearing the visage of death rather than of life. The next instant the House and galleries burst into a deafening clamor which rolled up and back in mighty waves that shook the very walls.

There was no stilling it. Again and again it burst forth, the mingling of ten thousand words, howling, rumbling, and groaning like the warring elements of nature. Several times the president stretched forth his great white hands appealing for silence, while the dew of mingled dread and anguish beaded on his brow and trickled down his cheeks in liquid supplication that his people might either slay him or listen to him.

The tumult stilled its fury for a moment, and he could be heard saying brokenly: "My countrymen, oh, my countrymen—"

But the quick sharp sound of the gavel cut him short. "The president must withdraw," said the Speaker, calmly and coldly, "his presence here is a menace to our free deliberation."

Again the tumult set up its deafening roar, while a look of almost horror overspread the countenance of the chief magistrate.

Once more his great white hands went heavenward, pleading for silence with such a mute majesty of supplication, that silence fell upon the immense assemblage, and his lips moved not in vain.

"Gentlemen of the House of Representatives, I stand here upon my just and lawful right as president of the republic, to give you 'information of the state of the Union.' I have summoned the honorable Senate, to meet me in this chamber. I call upon you to calm your passions and give ear to me as your oath of office sets the sacred obligation upon you."

There was a tone of godlike authority in these few words, almost divine enough to make the winds obey and still the tempestuous sea.

In deepest silence, and with a certain show of rude and native grandeur of bearing, the senators made their entrance into the chamber, the members of the House rising, and the Speaker advancing to meet the vice president.

The spectacle was grand and moving. Tears gathered in eyes long unused to them, and at an almost imperceptible nod of the president's head, the chaplain raised his voice in prayer. He prayed in accents that were so gentle and so persuasive, they must have turned the hardest heart to blessed thoughts of peace and love and fraternity and union.

And then again, all eyes were fixed with intense strain upon the face of the president.

"Gentlemen of the House of Representatives, this measure upon which you are now deliberating…"

With a sudden blow that startled every living soul within its hearing, the Speaker's gavel fell. "The President," said he with a superb dignity that called down from the galleries a burst of deafening applause, "must not make reference to pending legislation.

"The Constitution guarantees him the right 'from time to time to give to the Congress information of the Union.' He must keep himself strictly within the lines of this constitutional limit or withdraw from the bar of the House."

A deadly pallor overspread the face of the chief magistrate till it seemed he must sink then and there into that sleep which knows no awakening, but he gasped, he leaned forward, he raised his hand again imploringly, and as he did so, the bells of the city began to toll the hour of midnight.

The new year, the new century, was born, but with the last stroke, a fearful and thunderous discharge as of a thousand monster pieces of artillery, shook the Capitol to its very foundations, making the stoutest hearts stand still, and blanching checks that had never known the coward color.

The dome of the Capitol had been destroyed by dynamite. In a few moments, when it was seen that the chamber had suffered no harm, the leader of the House moved the final passage of the act.

The president was led away, and the Republican senators and representatives passed slowly out of the disfigured Capitol, while the tellers prepared to take the vote of the House.

The bells were ringing glad welcome to the new century, but a solemn tolling would have been a fitter thing, for the republic of Washington was no more.

It had died so peacefully that the world could not believe the tidings of its passing away.

As the dawn broke cold and gray, and its first dim light fell upon that shattered dome, glorious even in its ruins, a single human eye, filled with a gleam of devilish joy, looked up at it long and steadily, and then its owner was caught up and lost in the surging mass of humanity that held the Capitol girt round and round.

1900 or The Last President concludes.

Differing Philosophies:
The Fundamental Cause of Division

It is difficult to imagine how Lockwood might have done any better job of outlining the fault lines between today's political Left and Right than what he has laid out in this modest work of his.

In just a few short pages, he presented many of the familiar flashpoints separating the two divergent paths being laid out for America's future.

Perhaps not surprisingly, the flashpoints set out in this book follow the same points of tension where Donald Trump's America-First and Make-America-Great-Again visions cut against the unifying global visions of Build Back Better echoed not only by Joe Biden, but by Trudeau, Boris Johnson, and others...right up to Klaus Schwab.

Although the "personality" differences between Republicans and Democrats may be baffling to some, the explanation is not that complicated. Those differences flow directly out of the philosophical orientation of each party. The growing hostility between them shouldn't surprise any of us.

After all, unlike conflicts over superficial things like money, the battleground over which they are fighting is an actual zero-sum game. In the question of power, who gets to decide?

Does our world consist of free men and women who should have as much autonomy as a free society can allow without that freedom causing a loss of cohesion? Or does it consist of an endless array of competing interest groups whose collective interests need to be weighed off against one another by the arbitrary decisions of *someone in charge*?

While Joe Biden might stand at a podium and openly pretend to wonder what Republicans are "for," it isn't nearly the mystery he pretends it is.

Republicans think the Constitution, with the rights and protections described therein, forms an excellent framework for how to manage a country.

Republicans like checks and balances in a government to keep power from being concentrated too much in any one place.

Republicans like a small government held tightly on a short leash. We need look no further than our northern neighbor's Justin Trudeau to see what can go wrong when such safeguards are not cemented in place.

Conservatives press for a smaller government, with fewer levers of coercion and control within its reach. They prefer limitations on, for example, the state's police powers over the individual. The reason is simple: the more limited the scope of a government's power is, the fewer opportunities there will be for corrupt or ambitious politicians to color outside the lines.

Human history—especially the carefully recorded triumphs and failures of antiquity—have handed down many lessons about the limitations of human nature, and how easily power can be leveraged in dangerous ways.

It makes little difference in the end whether harm to a nation is done by a well-meaning incompetent or a self-serving autocrat, and so the political Right wants limited government.

Rights, from this perspective, mean the right for an individual not to be (unjustifiably) fleeced or controlled by governments, elected officials or bureaucrats in cubicles making arbitrary rules the free citizen must follow...or else.

This is not to say, as their critics suggest, they are trying to recapture one idyllic day, long ago, where everything was perfect. Even good things can be improved.

The birth of the GOP itself was established on the idea that freedoms already enjoyed by America's white citizens should also be extended to her black citizens. That emancipation made for a "more perfect" union.

It was a bold stand, but it was the natural outgrowth of this same political impulse—that all citizens should fully enjoy the rights (and obligations) of free men regardless of ethnic background.

The Democrats, by their nature, have a very different perspective. They are utopians. They lean into grand visions. Unlike the more pragmatic instincts of their counterparts, they are idealists. They tell one another grandiose stories about how wonderful life will be when their world-transforming systems can finally be put into place.

Unlike the conservatives, who have built-in practical limitations in just how far a limited government model can reduce the reach of political involvement in the life of the individual, the Left is playing a fundamentally different game.

Once you start increasing the role of government in an individual's life, an endless horizon of possibilities stretches out in front of you. You are limited only by your own imagination. Who could possibly have predicted, during the Clinton administration, that our government would have changed our working definition not only of marriage, but of gender itself?

Can you imagine meeting someone who had been in a coma since late 2019, and trying to explain how quickly the world devolved into an authoritarian biomedical state in the following three years, with people who had no signs of any actual illness being "quarantined" in their homes for weeks at a time?

Imagine explaining that churches and businesses were being arbitrarily shut down, and that anyone refusing to get an injection that had not been subjected to any long-term testing would be shunned out of polite society and forbidden to travel or eat inside a restaurant. Many would even be fired from their jobs for it. Companies would be permitted to discriminate against potential recruits based on their decision to abstain from it.

Previously unthinkable scenarios came from an elevation of the "experts" to positions of power the Framers would never have dreamed possible in our current system. The checks and balances broke down when an emergency was invoked.

Even without such unrestrained lawmaking power, the Constitution has often been reimagined in creative ways by Democrats to accommodate bold new initiatives.

For example, Obama explicitly stated he did not have the authority to unilaterally change immigration law. That didn't stop him from signing an executive order now understood as DACA—changing immigration law.

More recently, Biden understood that his administration lacked the authority to extend an eviction moratorium, or to issue a vaccine mandate through OSHA. Lacking any legal authority to perform an action didn't stop them from doing it anyway, and "nudging" employers to compel staff to get vaccinated or be fired.

But what happens when you give idealists who think they know better than the rest of us what system will "save" us and make life "better"? To borrow that Facebook slogan, they "move fast and break things." Forgiveness is so much easier to ask than permission. And blaming scapegoats is even better.

The plan is simple: push a change, make that change difficult to reverse, and *presto*, we're all stuck with something called the "new normal."

With the agenda-driven personalities in D.C., the rapid transformation from America First to the brand of globalism that came afterward with a stack of executive orders, and policies pushed by Biden, Pelosi, and Schumer in our generation was as predictable as it was ambitious.

The progressive Democrats in Lockwood's era were precisely the same sort of "visionaries" wanting to reimagine our world into a progressive fantasy today. Like Biden, they too hit the ground running, right from the beginning.

What they were not expecting was resistance from within their own party. Manchin's refusal to endorse their trillion-dollar agendas was the one thing that caught them off guard.

Whether it's Bryan, or Biden, or a network of billionaires talking grand strategy, the Left's utopian plan always works on the same model. It proposes a "common man" (or victim group, or minority) who has been marginalized.

That group, inevitably, is held up as the special-interest group needing to be rescued by some powerful political savior. This is why it's so important for Democrats to throw around us-versus-them language, and demonize the political Right as unthinking, unfeeling, and hostile to...whichever political interest group is currently in fashion.

Even within the pages of this book, we see how Democrats were supposedly going to bring newfound prosperity to the black man, just so long as he didn't get anywhere close to holding power in his own right.

Remember the major player mentioned in chapter 4? It was "Pitchfork Ben" Tillman. He was no ordinary white supremacist. Tillman counted personal participation in antiblack racial violence among his proudest moments. The Jim Crow South could never have been the same without the influence of the prominent Democrat who once said, "We of the South have never recognized the right of the Negro to govern white men, and we never will."

This comes back to the big lie buried in the heart of the doctrine of Marxist identarian movements like the one that has seized the American Left.

They claim to offer big solutions to special interest groups among Americans who have been sorted into categories of oppressor and oppressed. The oppressed/oppressor language used back in Lockwood's day is still being used to divide Americans in today's political campaigns.

The Left makes a big deal about caring for interest groups, despite a track record of failing the individuals within those groups at a profound level. And why wouldn't they? The minute individuals within those artificial victim groups stop seeing themselves as victims, they will no longer need help from that unspoken third category of group: the political rescuer.

This is part of why Trump's presidency was such a threat. Not only did he go into "hard" districts that Republicans had all but ignored in the past as "lost causes," but he issued a challenge to minority groups who had reflexively voted for the other team. "What have you got to lose?"

Then Trump took office and made good on those promises. Every single demographic shattered employment numbers. If the "China virus" hadn't shut down the economy, a 2020 reelection would have been an absolute cakewalk.

The MAGA vision for helping the ordinary citizen included practical policy changes that benefit the most possible people, taking power and control out of the government's hands (for example: the systematic slashing of red tape) to free the individual or business to do what they do best.

The Build-Back-Better version reverses that power shift, centralizing more power in the hands of fewer people...to the point that they are even pushing to *federalize* state elections for the "oppressed minority," of course.

In the process of all their extra spending, red tape, and excessive regulation, Biden's Democrats have triggered exactly the negative consequences conservatives had predicted, including fewer jobs and rampant inflation.

In reality, as in this book, we are faced with a hard choice between mutually exclusive alternatives.

On one side stands the promise of Bryan, Biden, AOC, and Vladimir Lenin...the promise that the government has limitless resources to provide each and every need the citizen could possibly want—so long as it squeezes the right citizens and businesses hard enough to pay their "fair share."

This was Lenin's "Peace. Land. Bread" promise. It's Bernie Sanders' free education promise. And it's the socialism that Joe Biden affirms with every radical he appoints to government positions. They hope you never clue in that their promise is the same "safe" comfort promised by the zookeeper and the prison guard.

On the other side stands the promise made in the speeches of such presidents as George Washington, John F. Kennedy, Ronald Reagan, and Donald J. Trump. They offer no assurances, for life offers no guarantees. They promise only opportunity.

In place of bland promises of peace, land, bread, their pitch is something grander and nobler: life, liberty, and the pursuit of happiness.

When Donald Trump stood up and pledged America would never become a socialist country, there was an aspect of that statement that was an expression of his will and determination. But there was something more to it.

He believed, as we do, that if Americans can look with clear-eyed understanding upon the options presented before us, we cannot but choose a grand and risky freedom over a pale and groveling certainty, ninety-nine times out of a hundred.

Such clarity was the objective of this book. We can but hope it has served our readers well in that humble purpose.

Afterword

—Brandon Vallorani

Liz and I have a higher purpose for writing this book alongside Ingersoll's original allegory. It was not simply to frighten the reader. It was to issue a clear prophetic warning and offer a solution. Identifying the problem is the first step toward developing that solution.

The temporary fix is to elect constitutional, God-fearing leaders to office in the next election cycle. But even the next election cycle is just that. A cycle. Even if we win the next election, will conservatives continue to win long-term? Only if we win the hearts and minds of the American people.

We know the Left will continue its attack on American values and our way of life until there is nothing left of our beloved country. There is a lasting and long-term solution that I must share with you now.

We must first recognize that America's problems are spiritual rather than merely political. As the late Andrew Breitbart said, politics are downstream of culture. I will take it back one step and suggest that culture is downstream of our faith. A secular religion creates a secular culture, which creates secular politics. A Christian faith creates a Christian culture, which creates Christian politics.

This begs the question, what happened to America's faith? America was founded as a Christian nation and has been blessed for generations because of it. Over the past two and a half centuries, however, Christians slowly began to pull out of society and retreat into the four walls of the church.

The rise of dispensational theology in the late 19th century caused many Christians to begin looking to the sky for a heavenly escape and as a result, abdicate their role in shepherding society. This is not what our pilgrim forefathers believed when they sailed from England to America in 1620. Thank God for their vision!

At one time, I believed that we were living in the last days of human history and that Jesus was going to return at any moment to rapture His church and judge the world. I grew up in the '70s, when apocalyptic books like *The Late Great Planet Earth* by Hal Lindsey were taking the American church by storm. In addition to hundreds of sermons on the subject, I remember quite vividly the time our church played the *Thief in the Night* film series. In case you don't remember, the series consisted of the following frightening films: *A Thief in the Night*, *A Distant Thunder*, *Image of the Beast*, and *Prodigal Planet*.

The powerful and terrifying concept of an imminent apocalypse defined my view of Christianity well into my married years. And as much as it may have helped me to develop a fear of God, it ultimately left me with many unanswered questions. Questions like, why did the New Testament writers always refer to the coming of Christ as being near and in their lifetime? And why does the book of Revelation say that the events of the book are "at hand" and will "shortly come to pass?"

I pondered the question, "If the Bible is inspired by God, which it is, why didn't the writers understand that the return of Christ would be two thousand plus years later?" Furthermore, why would Christ establish a church in the 1st century that was doomed to deteriorate and fail a mere twenty centuries later?

Late nights watching Jack Van Impe and John Hagee, with their elaborate prophetic charts and graphs and no real alternative, kept me locked into a downward spiraling system. The more complicated the story, the more convincing it became.

My apocalyptic house of cards finally collapsed, however, when I watched a video called *Demystifying Revelation* featuring Gary DeMar, Ken Gentry, and Ralph Barker in the year

2000. I remember the incredible boost of faith I received when I heard them say that the Bible meant exactly what it said when it referred to the timing of Christ's return. Using history, they showed me how most of the prophetic events of the Bible were fulfilled with stunning accuracy in the years leading up to and including the destruction of Jerusalem in A.D. 70.

I urge you take off your "last days" glasses for just a moment and read the following verses again:

> Matthew 16:27–28 (NIV) For the Son of Man is going to come in his Father's glory with his angels, and then he will reward each person according to what they have done. Truly I tell you, some who are standing here will not taste

death before they see the Son of Man coming in his kingdom.

Matthew 10:23 (NIV) When you are persecuted in one place, flee to another. Truly I tell you, you will not finish going through the towns of Israel before the Son of Man comes.

Matthew 24:29–34 (NIV) Immediately after the distress of those days "the sun will be darkened, and the moon will not give its light; the stars will fall from the sky, and the heavenly bodies will be shaken." [Isaiah 13:10; 34:4]

Then will appear the sign of the Son of Man in heaven. And then all the peoples of the earth [the tribes of the land] will mourn when they see the Son of Man coming on the clouds of heaven, with power and great glory. [Daniel 7:13–14]

And he will send his angels with a loud trumpet call, and they will gather his elect from the four winds, from one end of the heavens to the other. Now learn this lesson from the fig tree: As soon as its twigs get tender and its leaves come out, you know that summer is near. Even so, when you see all these things, you know that it [he] is near, right at the door.

Truly I tell you, this generation will certainly not pass away until all these things have happened. Romans 16:20 (NIV) The God of peace will soon crush Satan under your feet. The grace of our Lord Jesus be with you.

Hebrews 10:37 (NIV) For, "In just a little while, he who is coming will come and will not delay."

James 5:7-9 (NIV) "Be patient, then, brothers and sisters, until the Lord's coming. See how the farmer waits for the land to yield its valuable crop, patiently waiting for the autumn and spring rains. You too, be patient and stand firm, because the Lord's coming is near.

9 Don't grumble against one another, brothers and sisters, or you will be judged. The Judge is standing at the door!"

1 John 2:18 (NIV) Dear children, this is the last hour; and as you have heard that the antichrist is coming, even now many antichrists have come. This is how we know it is the last hour.

Revelation 1:1 (NIV) The revelation from Jesus Christ, which God gave him to show his servants what must soon take place. He made it known by sending his angel to his servant John,

Revelation 1:3 (NIV) Blessed is the one who reads aloud the words of this prophecy, and blessed are those who hear it and take to heart what is written in it, because the time is near.

Revelation 22:6–7 (NIV) The angel said to me, "These words are trustworthy and true. The Lord, the God who inspires the prophets, sent his angel to show his servants the things that must soon take place."

"Look, I am coming soon! Blessed is the one who keeps the words of the prophecy written in this scroll."
Revelation 22:10 (NIV) Then he told me, "Do not seal up the words of the prophecy of this scroll, because the time is near.

If the Bible is the infallible word of God, which it is, can this many passages inaccurately predict the timing of Christ's return? I believe absolutely not.

Let's be honest with the text. Matthew 24:34, for example, requires that the great tribulation occur before the current generation (about forty years) passed away. Add approximately forty years to A.D. 33, and you'll find yourself in the midst of one of the most horrific events in history: the crucifixion of millions of Jews, the destruction of the temple, and the burning of the Holy City of Jerusalem. The entire old covenant system collapsed at that time. Not a single sacrifice has been offered by the Jewish people since that time. Most people fail to realize that this was perhaps the most significant event in prophetic history.

I know you're skeptical and have a lot of questions, so I highly encourage you to read *Is Jesus Coming Soon?* and *Last Days Madness* by Gary DeMar, for more information. His ability to interpret the Bible plainly and his clear writing style will captivate you and build your faith.

If the great tribulation was a past event, what about the return of Christ?

In Matthew 24:30, Jesus states: "Then will appear the sign of the Son of Man in heaven. And then all the peoples of the earth will mourn when they see the Son of Man coming on the clouds of heaven, with power and great glory"

Most Christians believe this is referring to the Second Coming of Christ. But is it? Jesus is actually quoting directly from Daniel 7:13–14, which reads:

> In my vision at night I looked, and there before me was one like a son of man, coming with the clouds of heaven. He approached the Ancient of Days and was led into his presence. He was given authority, glory and sovereign power; all nations and peoples of every language worshiped him. His dominion is an everlasting dominion that will not pass away, and his kingdom is one that will never be destroyed.

It is clear that this passage teaches that Jesus is going up in the clouds of heaven and *not* coming down to earth. He is going to God the Father, who will give Him an everlasting kingdom. This event must have happened before A.D. 70, because Jesus said that the entire Olivet discourse would be fulfilled before this generation passed away.

It is true that Christ will one day return to earth bodily (1 Thess. 4:16) and defeat his final enemy, which is death (1 Corinthians 15:25–26). Until then, he is reigning in heaven on the throne of His Father David (Acts 2:33–36 and Heb. 1). If most prophecy has been fulfilled, now what?

Is there anything left to happen on God's prophetic calendar? You bet. The darkest part of human history is over.

We now have the hope of a growing and expanding kingdom already underway!

In the book of Daniel, we are given a vivid picture of the timing, power, and scope of Christ's kingdom. Daniel 2 tells us about the dream King Nebuchadnezzar had of the great image made of gold, silver, bronze, iron, and clay. Daniel interprets the image as representing four kingdoms that would rule on the earth: Babylon, Medo-Persia, Greece, and Rome. Incidentally, this passage does not teach that there will be a second or "revived" Roman empire in the future.

The stone that crushes the image in verses thirty-four through thirty-five represents Christ's kingdom. In Daniel 2:44, Daniel states that in the days of the fourth kingdom (Rome), "the God of heaven will set up a kingdom which shall never be destroyed; and the kingdom shall not be left to other people; it shall break in pieces and consume all these kingdoms, and it shall stand forever."

Hundreds of years after Daniel made this remarkable prophecy, John the Baptist arrives on the scene, during the Roman empire, and calls people to, "Repent, for the kingdom of heaven is at hand!" Of course, Jesus also taught that His kingdom was about to be inaugurated. In Matthew 4:17, Jesus also states, "Repent: for the kingdom of heaven is at hand."

The kingdom of God is growing, and we've only just begun. In Deuteronomy 7:9, God promises that his love and faithfulness will extend to a thousand generations. And Galatians 3 reminds us that all those who have faith in Christ are heir to the promises of Israel. If a generation is about forty years, then we've only completed about six thousand years of history and have at least thirty-four thousand years to go! We're not living in the last days—we're living in the exciting days of the early church!

Every decision we make today, especially how we train our children, will make an impact for thousands of years to come. God has given us an opportunity to make a tremendous impact for His kingdom.

This is an exciting time to be alive in history. Don't get caught up in the doom and gloom sensationalism of the liberal media and prophecy writers. Instead, think about your grandchildren's grandchildren. What kind of a vision will you leave them with after your passing?

For more information on the growing Kingdom of Christ, I encourage you to read *Postmillennialism: An Eschatology of Hope* by Keith Matthison.

The most appropriate way to end this book is to chant the motto of the Revolutionary War, "No king but King Jesus!"

Appendix A:
Plessy v. Ferguson (1896)

The ruling in this Supreme Court case upheld a Louisiana state law that allowed for "equal but separate accommodations for the white and colored races."

During the era of Reconstruction, black Americans' political rights were affirmed by three constitutional amendments and numerous laws passed by Congress. Racial discrimination was attacked on a particularly broad front by the Civil Rights Act of 1875. This legislation made it a crime for an individual to deny "the full and equal enjoyment of any of the accommodations, advantages, facilities, and privileges of inns, public conveyances on land or water, theaters and other places of public amusement; subject only to the conditions and limitations established by law, and applicable alike to citizens of every race and color."

In 1883, the Supreme Court struck down the 1875 act, ruling that the 14th Amendment did not give Congress authority to prevent discrimination by private individuals. Victims of racial discrimination were told to seek relief not from the federal government, but from the states. At the same time, state governments were passing legislation that codified inequality between the races. Laws requiring the establishment of separate schools for children of each race were most common; however, segregation was soon extended to most public and semipublic facilities through "Jim Crow" laws.

Beginning with passage of an 1887 Florida law, states began to require that railroads furnish separate accommodations for each race. These measures were unpopular with the railway companies that bore the expense of adding Jim Crow cars. Segregation of the railroads was even more objectionable to black citizens, who saw it as a further step toward the total repudiation of three constitutional amendments. When such a bill was proposed before the Louisiana legislature in 1890, the black community of New Orleans protested vigorously. Nonetheless, despite the presence of sixteen black legislators in the state assembly, the law was passed. It required either separate passenger coaches or partitioned coaches to provide segregated accommodations for each race. Passengers were required to sit in the appropriate areas or face a twenty-five-dollar fine or a twenty-day jail sentence. Black nurses attending white children were permitted to ride in white compartments, however.

In 1891, a group of concerned young black men of New Orleans formed the "Citizens' Committee to Test the Constitutionality of the Separate Car Law." They raised money and engaged Albion W. Tourgée, a prominent radical Republican author and politician, as their lawyer. On May 15, 1892, the Louisiana State Supreme Court decided in favor of the Pullman Company's claim that the law was unconstitutional as it applied to interstate travel. Encouraged, the committee decided to press a test case on intrastate travel. With the cooperation of the East Louisiana Railroad, on June 7, 1892, Homer Plessy, a mulatto (7/8 white), seated himself in a white compartment, was challenged by the conductor, and was arrested and charged with violating the state law. In the criminal district court for the parish of Orleans, Tourgée argued that the law requiring "separate but equal accommodations" was unconstitutional. When Judge John H. Ferguson ruled against him, Plessy applied to the state supreme court for a writ of prohibition and certiorari. Although the court upheld the state law, it granted Plessy's petition for a writ of error that would enable him to appeal the case to the Supreme Court.

In 1896, the Supreme Court issued its decision in *Plessy v. Ferguson*. Justice Henry Brown of Michigan delivered the majority opinion, which sustained the constitutionality of Louisiana's Jim Crow law. In part, he said:

> We consider the underlying fallacy of the plaintiff's argument to consist in the assumption that the enforced separation of the two races stamps the colored race with a badge of inferiority. If this be so, it is not by reason of anything found in the act, but solely because the colored race chooses to put that construction upon it.... The argument also assumes that social prejudice may be overcome by legislation, and that equal rights cannot be secured except by an enforced commingling of the two races.... If the civil and political rights of both races be equal, one cannot be inferior to the other civilly

or politically. If one race be inferior to the other socially, the Constitution of the United States cannot put them upon the same plane.

In the lone dissent, Kentuckian Justice John Marshall Harlan wrote:

> I am of the opinion that the statute of Louisiana is inconsistent with the personal liberties of citizens, white and black, in that State, and hostile to both the spirit and the letter of the Constitution of the United States. If laws of like character should be enacted in the several States of the Union, the effect would be in the highest degree mischievous. Slavery as an institution tolerated by law would, it is true, have disappeared from our country, but there would remain a power in the States, by sinister legislation, to interfere with the blessings of freedom; to regulate civil rights common to all citizens, upon the basis of race; and to place in a condition of legal inferiority a large body of American citizens, now constituting a part of the political community, called the people of the United States, for whom and by whom, through representatives, our government is administrated. Such a system is inconsistent with the guarantee given by the Constitution to each State of a republican form of government, and may be stricken down by congressional action, or by the courts in the

discharge of their solemn duty to maintain the supreme law of the land, anything in the Constitution or laws of any State to the contrary notwithstanding.

It was not until the Supreme Court's decision in *Brown v. Board of Education* and congressional civil rights acts of the 1950s and 1960s that systematic segregation under state law was ended. In the wake of those federal actions, many states amended or rewrote their state constitutions to conform with the spirit of the 14th Amendment. For Homer Plessy, the remedies came too late.[2]

Appendix B:
William Jennings Bryan's
"Cross of Gold" Speech

The most famous speech in American political history was delivered by William Jennings Bryan on July 9, 1896, at the Democratic National Convention in Chicago. The topic was whether to endorse the free coinage of silver at a ratio of silver to gold of sixteen to one. This inflationary measure would have increased the amount of money in circulation and aided cash-poor and debt-burdened farmers. After speeches on the subject by several U.S. senators, Bryan rose to speak. The thirty-six-year-old former Congressman from Nebraska aspired to be the Democratic nominee for president, and he had been skillfully, but quietly, building support for himself among the delegates. His dramatic speaking style and rhetoric roused the crowd to a frenzy. The response, wrote one reporter, "came like one great burst of artillery." Men and women screamed and waved their hats and canes. "Some," wrote another reporter, "like demented things, divested themselves of their coats and flung them high in the air." The next day the convention nominated Bryan for president on the fifth ballot.

I would be presumptuous, indeed, to present myself against the distinguished gentlemen to whom you have listened if this were but a measuring of ability; but this is not a contest among persons. The humblest citizen in all the land when clad in the armor of a righteous cause is stronger than all the whole hosts of error that they can bring. I come to speak to you in defense of a cause as holy as the cause of liberty—the cause of humanity. When this debate is concluded, a motion will be made to lay upon the table the resolution offered in commendation of the administration and also the resolution in condemnation of the administration. I shall object to bringing this question down to a level of persons. The individual is but an atom; he is born, he acts, he dies; but principles are eternal; and this has been a contest of principle.

Never before in the history of this country has there been witnessed such a contest as that through which we have passed. Never before in the history of American politics has a great issue been fought out as this issue has been by the voters themselves.

On the 4th of March, 1895, a few Democrats, most of them members of Congress, issued an address to the Democrats of the nation asserting that the money question was the paramount issue of the hour; asserting also the right of a majority of the

Democratic Party to control the position of the party on this paramount issue; concluding with the request that all believers in free coinage of silver in the Democratic Party should organize and take charge of and control the policy of the Democratic Party. Three months later, at Memphis, an organization was perfected, and the silver Democrats went forth openly and boldly and courageously proclaiming their belief and declaring that if successful they would crystallize in a platform the declaration which they had made; and then began the conflict with a zeal approaching the zeal which inspired the crusaders who followed Peter the Hermit. Our silver Democrats went forth from victory unto victory, until they are assembled now, not to discuss, not to debate, but to enter up the judgment rendered by the plain people of this country.

But in this contest, brother has been arrayed against brother, and father against son. The warmest ties of love and acquaintance and association have been disregarded. Old leaders have been cast aside when they refused to give expression to the sentiments of those whom they would lead, and new leaders have sprung up to give direction to this cause of freedom. Thus has the contest been waged, and we have assembled here under as binding and solemn instructions as were ever fastened upon the representatives of a people.

We do not come as individuals. Why, as individuals we might have been glad to compliment the gentleman from New York [Senator Hill], but we knew that the people for whom we speak would never be willing to put him in a position where he could thwart the will of the Democratic Party. I say it was not a question of persons; it was a question of principle; and it is not with gladness, my friends, that we find ourselves brought into conflict with those who are now arrayed on the other side. The gentleman who just preceded me [Governor Russell] spoke of the old state of Massachusetts. Let me assure him that not one person in all this convention entertains the least hostility to the people of the state of Massachusetts.

But we stand here representing people who are the equals before the law of the largest cities in the state of Massachusetts. When you come before us and tell us that we shall disturb your business interests, we reply that you have disturbed our business interests by your action. We say to you that you have made too limited in its application the definition of a businessman. The man who is employed for wages is as much a businessman as his employer. The attorney in a country town is as much a businessman as the corporation counsel in a great metropolis. The merchant at the crossroads store is as much a businessman as the merchant of New York. The farmer who goes forth in the morning and toils all day, begins in the spring and toils all summer, and by the application of brain and muscle to the natural resources of this country creates wealth, is as much a businessman as the man who goes upon the Board of Trade and bets upon the price of grain. The miners who go 1,000 feet into the earth or climb 2,000 feet upon the cliffs and bring forth from their hiding places the precious metals to be poured in the channels of trade are as much businessmen as the few financial magnates who in a backroom corner the money of the world.

We come to speak for this broader class of businessmen. Ah. my friends, we say not one word against those who live upon the Atlantic Coast; but those hardy pioneers who braved all the dangers of the wilderness, who have made the desert to blossom as the rose—those pioneers away out there, rearing their children near to nature's heart, where they can mingle their voices with the voices of the birds—out there where they have erected schoolhouses for the education of their children and churches where they praise their Creator, and the cemeteries where sleep the ashes of their dead—are as deserving of the consideration of this party as any people in this country.

It is for these that we speak. We do not come as aggressors. Our war is not a war of conquest. We are fighting in the defense of our homes, our families, and posterity. We have petitioned, and our petitions have been scorned. We have entreated, and our entreaties have been disregarded. We have begged, and they have mocked when our calamity came.

We beg no longer; we entreat no more; we petition no more. We defy them!

The gentleman from Wisconsin has said he fears a Robespierre. My friend, in this land of the free you need fear no tyrant who will spring up from among the people. What we need is an Andrew Jackson to stand as Jackson stood, against the encroachments of aggregated wealth.

They tell us that this platform was made to catch votes. We reply to them that changing conditions make new issues; that the principles upon which rest Democracy are as everlasting as the hills; but that they must be applied to new conditions as they arise. Conditions have arisen and we are attempting to meet those conditions. They tell us that the income tax ought not to be brought in here; that is not a new idea. They criticize us for our criticism of the Supreme Court of the United States. My friends, we have made no criticism. We have simply called attention to what you know. If you want criticisms, read the dissenting opinions of the Court. That will give you criticisms.

They say we passed an unconstitutional law. I deny it. The income tax was not unconstitutional when it was passed. It was not unconstitutional when it went before the Supreme Court for the first time. It did not become unconstitutional until one judge changed his mind; and we cannot be expected to know when a judge will change his mind.

The income tax is a just law. It simply intends to put the burdens of government justly upon the backs of the people. I am in favor of an income tax. When I find a man who is not willing to pay his share of the burden of the government which protects him, I find a man who is unworthy to enjoy the blessings of a government like ours.

He says that we are opposing the national bank currency. It is true. If you will read what Thomas Benton said, you will find that he said that in searching history he could find but one parallel to Andrew Jackson. That was Cicero, who destroyed the conspiracies of Cataline and saved Rome. He did for Rome what Jackson did when he destroyed the bank conspiracy and saved America.

We say in our platform that we believe that the right to coin money and issue money is a function of government. We believe it. We believe it is a part of sovereignty and can no more with safety be delegated to private individuals than can the power to make penal statutes or levy laws for taxation.

Mr. Jefferson, who was once regarded as good Democratic authority, seems to have a different opinion from the gentleman who has addressed us on the part of the minority. Those who are opposed to this proposition tell us that the issue of paper money is a function of the bank, and that the government ought to go out of the banking business. I stand with Jefferson rather than with them, and tell them, as he did, that the issue of money is a function of the government and that the banks should go out of the governing business.

They complain about the plank which declares against the life tenure in office. They have tried to strain it to mean that which it does not mean. What we oppose in that plank is the life tenure that is being built up in Washington which establishes an office-holding class and excludes from participation in the benefits the humbler members of our society....

Let me call attention to two or three great things. The gentleman from New York says that he will propose an amendment providing that this change in our law shall not affect contracts which, according to the present laws, are made payable in gold. But if he means to say that we cannot change our monetary system without protecting those who have loaned money before the change was made, I want to ask him where, in law or in morals, he can find authority for not protecting the debtors when the act of 1873 was passed when he now insists that we must protect the creditor. He says he also wants to amend this platform so as to provide that if we fail to maintain the parity within a year that we will then suspend the coinage of silver. We reply that when we advocate a thing which we believe will be successful we are not compelled to raise a doubt as to our own sincerity by trying to show what we will do if we are wrong.

I ask him, if he will apply his logic to us, why he does not apply it to himself. He says that he wants this country to try to secure an international agreement. Why doesn't he tell us what he is going to do if they fail to secure an international agreement. There is more reason for him to do that than for us to expect to fail to maintain the parity. They have tried for thirty years—thirty years—to secure an international agreement, and those are waiting for it most patiently who don't want it at all.

Now, my friends, let me come to the great paramount issue. If they ask us here why it is we say more on the money question than we say upon the tariff question, I reply that if protection has slain its thousands the gold standard has slain its tens of thousands. If they ask us why we did not embody all these things in our platform which we believe, we reply to them that when we have restored the money of the Constitution, all other necessary reforms will be possible, and that until that is done there is no reform that can be accomplished.

Why is it that within three months such a change has come over the sentiments of the country? Three months ago, when it was confidently asserted that those who believed in the gold standard would frame our platforms and nominate our candidates, even the advocates of the gold standard did not think that we could elect a President; but they had good reasons for the suspicion, because there is scarcely a state here today asking for the gold standard that is not within the absolute control of the Republican Party.

But note the change. Mr. McKinley was nominated at St. Louis upon a platform that declared for the maintenance of the gold standard until it should be changed into bimetallism by an international agreement. Mr. McKinley was the most popular man among the Republicans; and everybody three months ago in the Republican Party prophesied his election. How is it today? Why, that man who used to boast that he looked like Napoleon, that man shudders today when he thinks that he was nominated on the anniversary of the Battle of Waterloo. Not only that, but as he listens, he can hear with ever increasing distinctness the sound of the waves as they beat upon the lonely shores of St. Helena.

Why this change? Ah, my friends. is not the change evident to anyone who will look at the matter? It is because no private character, however pure, no personal popularity, however great, can protect from the avenging wrath of an indignant people the man who will either declare that he is in favor of fastening the gold standard upon this people, or who is willing to surrender the right of self-government and place legislative control in the hands of foreign potentates and powers....

We go forth confident that we shall win. Why? Because upon the paramount issue in this campaign there is not a spot of ground upon which the enemy will dare to challenge battle. Why, if they tell us that the gold standard is a good thing, we point to their platform and tell them that their platform pledges the party to get rid of a gold standard and substitute bimetallism. If the gold standard is a good thing, why try to get rid of it? If the gold standard, and I might call your attention to the fact that some of the very people who are in this convention today and who tell you that we ought to declare in favor of international bimetallism and thereby declare that the gold standard is wrong and that the principles of bimetallism are better—these very people four months ago were open and avowed advocates of the gold standard and telling us that we could not legislate two metals together even with all the world.

I want to suggest this truth, that if the gold standard is a good thing we ought to declare in favor of its retention and not in favor of abandoning it; and if the gold standard is a bad thing, why should we wait until some other nations are willing to help us to let it go?

Here is the line of battle. We care not upon which issue they force the fight. We are prepared to meet them on either issue or on both. If they tell us that the gold standard is the standard of civilization, we reply to them that this, the most enlightened of all nations of the earth, has never declared for a gold standard, and both the parties this year are declaring against it. If the gold standard is the standard of civilization, why, my friends, should we not have it? So if they come to meet us on that, we can present the history of our nation. More than that, we can tell them this, that they will search the pages of history in vain to find a single instance in which the common people of any land ever declared themselves in favor of a gold standard. They can find where the holders of fixed investments have.

Mr. Carlisle said in 1878 that this was a struggle between the idle holders of idle capital and the struggling masses who produce the wealth and pay the taxes of the country; and my friends, it is simply a question that we shall decide upon which side shall the Democratic Party fight. Upon the side of the idle holders of idle capital, or upon the side of the struggling masses? That is the question that the party must answer first; and then it must be answered by each individual hereafter. The sympathies of the Democratic Party, as described by the platform, are on the side of the struggling masses, who have ever been the foundation of the Democratic Party.

There are two ideas of government. There are those who believe that if you just legislate to make the well-to-do prosperous, that their prosperity will leak through on those below. The Democratic idea has been that if you legislate to make the masses prosperous their prosperity will find its way up and through every class that rests upon it.

You come to us and tell us that the great cities are in favor of the gold standard. I tell you that the great cities rest upon these broad and fertile prairies. Burn down your cities and leave our farms, and your cities will spring up again as if by magic. But destroy our farms and the grass will grow in the streets of every city in the country.

My friends, we shall declare that this nation is able to legislate for its own people on every question without waiting for the aid or consent of any other nation on earth, and upon that issue we expect to carry every single state in the Union.

I shall not slander the fair state of Massachusetts nor the state of New York by saying that when citizens are confronted with the proposition, "Is this nation able to attend to its own business?"—I will not slander either one by saying that the people of those states will declare our helpless impotency as a nation to attend to our own business. It is the issue of 1776 over again. Our ancestors, when but 3 million, had the courage to declare their political independence of every other nation upon earth. Shall we, their descendants, when we have grown to 70 million, declare that we are less independent than our forefathers? No, my friends, it will never be the judgment of this people. Therefore, we care not upon what lines the battle is fought. If they say bimetallism is good but we cannot have it till some nation helps us, we reply that, instead of having a gold standard because England has, we shall restore bimetallism, and then let England have bimetallism because the United States have.

If they dare to come out in the open field and defend the gold standard as a good thing, we shall fight them to the uttermost, having behind us the producing masses of the nation and the world. Having behind us the commercial interests and the laboring interests and all the toiling masses, we shall answer their demands for a gold standard by saying to them, you shall not press down upon the brow of labor this crown of thorns. You shall not crucify mankind upon a cross of gold.[3]

Appendix C:
Democratic Party Platform
Adopted at Chicago, July 9, 1896

We, the Democrats of the United States in National Convention assembled, do reaffirm our allegiance to those great essential principles of justice and liberty upon which our institutions are founded, and which the Democratic Party has advocated from Jefferson's time to our own--freedom of speech, freedom of the press, freedom of conscience, the separation of personal rights, the equality of all citizens before the law, and the faithful observance of constitutional limitations.

During all these years the Democratic Party has resented the tendency of selfish interests to the centralization of government power, and steadfastly maintained the integrity of the dual scheme of government established by the founders of this republic of republics. Under its guidance and teachings the great principle of local self-government has found its best expression in the maintenance of the rights of States and in its assertion of the necessity of confining the general government to the exercise of the powers granted by the Constitution of the United States.

The Constitution of the United States guarantees to every citizen the rights of civil and religious liberty. The Democratic Party has always been the exponent of political liberty and religious freedom, and it renews its obligations and reaffirms its devotion to these fundamental principles of the Constitution.

The Money Question. Recognizing that the money question is paramount to all others at this time, we invite attention to the fact that the Federal Constitution names silver and gold together as the money metals of the United States, and that the first coinage law passed by Congress under the Constitution made the silver dollar the monetary unit of value and admitted gold to free coinage at a ratio based upon the silver dollar unit.

The Demonetization of Silver. We declare that the act of 1873 demonetizing silver without the knowledge or approval of the American people, has resulted in the appreciation of gold and a corresponding fall in the prices of commodities produced by the people; a heavy increase in the burden of taxation and of all debts, public and private; the enrichment of the money-lending class at home and abroad; prostration of industry and impoverishment of the people.

Opposed to the Gold Standard. We are unalterably opposed to monometallism, which has locked fast the prosperity of an industrial people in the paralysis of hard times. Gold monometallism is a British policy, and its adoption has brought other nations into financial servitude to London. It is not only un-American, but anti-American, and it can be fastened on the United States only by the stifling of that spirit and love of liberty which proclaimed our political independence in 1776 and won it in the War of the Revolution.

Free and Unlimited Coinage. We demand the free and unlimited coinage of both silver and gold at the present legal ratio of 16 to 1, without waiting for the aid or consent of any other nation. We demand that the standard silver dollar shall be a full legal tender, equally with gold, for all debts, public and private, and we favor such legislation as will prevent for the future the demonetization of any kind of legal-tender money by private contract.

We are opposed to the policy and practice of surrendering to the holders of obligations of the United States the option reserved by law to the Government of redeeming such obligations in either silver coin or gold coin.

Opposed to the Issue of Bonds. We are opposed to the issuing of interest-bearing bonds of the United States in time of peace and condemn the trafficking with banking syndicates, which, in exchange for bonds and at an enormous profit to themselves, supply the Federal Treasury with gold to maintain the policy of gold monometallism.

The Issue of Paper Money. Congress alone has the power to coin and issue money, and President Jackson declared that this power could not be delegated to corporations or individuals.

We, therefore, denounce the issuance of notes intended to circulate as money by national banks as in derogation of the Constitution, and we demand that all paper which is made a legal tender for public and private debts, or which is receivable for dues to the United States, shall be issued by the Government of the United States, and shall be redeemable in coin.

The Tariff. We hold that tariff duties should be levied for purposes of revenue, such duties to be so adjusted as to operate equally throughout the country and not discriminate between class or section, and that taxation should be limited by the needs of the Government honestly and economically administered. We denounce, as disturbing to business, the Republican threat to restore the McKinley law, which has been twice condemned by the people in national elections, and which, enacted under the false plea of protection to home industry, proved a prolific breeder of trusts and monopolies, enriched the few at the expense of the many, restricted trade and deprived the producers of the great American staples of access to their natural markets. Until the money question is settled, we are opposed to any agitation for further changes in our tariff laws, except such as are necessary to meet the deficit in revenue caused by the adverse decision of the Supreme Court on the income tax.

The Income Tax. But for the decision by the Supreme Court there would be no deficit in the revenue under the law passed by a Democratic Congress in strict pursuance of the uniform decisions of that court for nearly 100 years, that court having in that decision sustained constitutional objections to its enactment which had previously been overruled by the ablest judges who had ever sat on that bench. We declare that it is the duty of Congress to use all the constitutional power which remains after that decision, or which may come from its reversal by the court as it may hereafter be constituted, so that the burdens of taxations may be equally and impartially laid, to the end that wealth may bear its due proportion of the expenses of the Government.

Foreign Pauper Labor. We hold that the most efficient way of protecting American labor is to prevent the importation of foreign pauper labor to compete with it in the home market, and that the value of the home market to our American farmers and artisans is greatly reduced by a vicious monetary system, which depresses the prices of their products below the cost of production, and thus deprives them of the means of purchasing the products of our home manufacturers, and, as labor creates the wealth of the country, we demand the passage of such laws as may be necessary to protect in all its rights.

We are in favor of the arbitration of differences between employers engaged in inter-State commerce and their employees, and recommend such legislation as is necessary to carry out this principle.

The absorption of wealth by the few, the consolidation of our leading railroad systems and the formation of trusts and pools require a stricter control by the Federal Government of those arteries of commerce. We demand the enlargement of the powers of the Inter-State Commerce Commission and such restrictions and guarantees in the control of railroads as will protect the people from robbery and oppression.

Reduction in the Number of Offices. We denounce the profligate waste of the money wrung from the people by oppressive taxation and the lavish appropriations of recent Republican Congresses, which have kept taxes high, while the labor that pays them is unemployed, and the products of the people's toil are depressed in price till they no longer repay the cost of production. We demand a return to that simplicity and economy which befits a Democratic government, and a reduction in the number of useless offices, the salaries of which drain the substance of the people.

Contempts in Federal Courts. We denounce the arbitrary interference by Federal authorities in local affairs as a violation of the Constitution of the United States and a crime against free institutions, and we especially object to government by injunction as a new and highly dangerous form of oppression by which Federal judges, in contempt of the laws of the States and rights of citizens, become at once legislators, judges, and executioners, and we approve the bill passed by the last session of the United States Senate and now pending in the House of Representatives, relative to contempts in Federal Courts and providing trials by jury in certain cases of contempt.

The Pacific Railroad Funding Bill. No discrimination shall be indulged in by the Government of the United States in favor of any of its debtors. We approve of the refusal of the Fifty-third Congress to pass the Pacific Railroad Funding Bill and denounce the efforts of the present Republican Congress to enact a similar measure.

The Pensioners. Recognizing the just claims of deserving Union soldiers, we heartily endorse the rule of the present Commissioner of Pensions that no names shall be arbitrarily dropped from the pension rolls, and the fact of enlistment and service should be deemed conclusive evidence against disease and disability before enlistment.

Territories. We favor the admission of the Territories of New Mexico, Oklahoma and Arizona to the Union as States, and we favor the early admission of all the Territories having the necessary population and resources to entitle them to Statehood, and, while they remain Territories, we hold that the officials appointed to administer the government of any Territory, together with the District of Columbia and Alaska, should be bona fide residents of the Territory or District in which the duties are to be performed. The Democratic Party believes in home rule, and that all public lands of the United States should be appropriated to the establishment of free homes for American citizens.

We recommend that the Territory of Alaska be granted a Delegate in Congress, and that the general land and timber laws of the United States be extended to said Territory.

The Monroe Doctrine. The Monroe doctrine, as originally declared and as interpreted by succeeding Presidents, is a permanent part of the foreign policy of the United States and must at all times be maintained.

Sympathy for the Cubans. We extend our sympathy to the people of Cuba in their heroic struggle for liberty and independence.

Civil Service. We are opposed to life tenure in the public service. We favor appointments based upon merit, fixed terms of office, and such an administration of the Civil Service laws as will afford equal opportunities to all citizens of ascertained fitness.

Opposed to a third term. We declare it to be the unwritten law of this republic, established by custom and usage of 100 years, and sanctioned by the examples of the greatest and wisest of those who founded and have maintained our government, that no man should be eligible for a third term of the Presidential office.

Waterways. The federal government should care for and improve the Mississippi River and other great waterways of the republic, so as to secure for the interior States easy and cheap transportation to tide-water. When any waterway of the republic is of sufficient important to demand aid of the government, such aid should be extended upon a definite plan of continuous work until permanent improvement is secured.

Confiding in the justness of our cause and the necessity of its success at the polls, we submit the foregoing declaration of principles and purposes to the considerate judgment of the American people. We invite the support of all citizens who approve them and who desire to have them made effective through legislation for the relief of the people and the restoration of the country's prosperity.[4]

Endnotes

1   Nickie Louise, "40% of US Dollars in Existence Were Printed in the Last 12 Months: Is America Repeating the Same Mistake of 1921 Weimar Germany?" Tech Startups, May 22, 2021, https://techstartups.com/2021/05/22/40-us.

2   "Plessy v. Ferguson (1896)," National Archives, last accessed June 5, 2023, https://www.archives.gov/milestone-documents/plessy-v-ferguson.

3   *Official Proceedings of the Democratic National Convention Held in Chicago, Illinois, July 7, 8, 9, 10, and 11, 1896,* (Logansport, Indiana: 1896), 226–234. Reprinted in *The Annals of America, Vol. 12, 1895–1904: Populism, Imperialism, and Reform* (Chicago: Encyclopedia Britannica, Inc.: 1968), 100–105.

4   "Democratic Party Platform," Vassar College, 2000, last accessed June 5, 2023, http://projects.vassar.edu/1896/chicago-platform.html.

5   "Lockwood, Ingersoll, 1841-1918," Library of Congress, last accessed June 12, 2023, https://id.loc.gov/authorities/names/no98117684.html.

Acknowledgments

The completion of this book could not have been possible without the expertise, research, and editing of Wes and Karen Walker.

We would also like to thank Lita Sanders for her proof-reading and fact-checking skills, and Kate Post for her editing and review.

A debt of gratitude is owed to Anthony Ziccardi, for his publishing acumen and guidance.

Last but not least, we want to thank our parents who all four raised us to be thinkers, doers, and patriots.

About the Authors

Ingersoll Lockwood (1841–1918) was an American lawyer and writer. He wrote the *Baron Trump* novels (1889/1893) as well as the dystopian title *1900 or The Last President*, a play, and several nonfiction works (some under the pseudonym Irwin Longman). His father, Munson, was an intimate friend of Henry Clay, who helped to found the National Republican Party. Munson Lockwood achieved prominence during his military service and civic activism, raising funds for the Hungarian statesman and freedom fighter Lajos Kossuth, whose bust can be found in the United States Capitol. Like his father, Ingersoll Lockwood trained as a lawyer, but his first position was as a diplomat. Appointed consul to the Kingdom of Hanover by President Abraham Lincoln in 1862, he was the youngest member of the U.S. consular force at the time and served for four years. On his return to the United States, he established a legal practice with his older brother in New York City. By the 1880s, Ingersoll had established a parallel career as a lecturer and writer and died with no children or surviving heirs at the age of seventy-seven.[5]

Brandon Vallorani is a visionary leader skilled in marketing, brand building, and business management. An accomplished executive and entrepreneur, Brandon's background in graphic design, marketing, and management has resulted in continually increasing success for himself and many others. Author of *The Wolves and the Mandolin* (2017) and *Let's Go Brandon* (2022) and coauthor of *Would Jesus Vote for Trump?* (2019), Vallorani is the founder of several brands and businesses, which achieved Inc. 5000 rankings six times. Vallorani resides in Metro Atlanta where he consults and oversees several conservative e-commerce operations (PatriotDepot.com, PatriotGear.com, Store.FlagandCross.com, MAGAfun.com), a premium cigar line (ValloraniCigars.com), a coffee shop in downtown Hiram, Georgia (PatriotFuel.com), and publishes the 1599 Geneva Bible (GenevaBible.com). He earned his MBA from Thomas More University in 2003 and his BFA in graphic design from West Virginia University in 1996.

Liz Martin is a fractional executive, having worked with visionary Brandon Vallorani for over fifteen years in publishing, e-commerce, marketing, brand building, and business development. Through Invicta Consulting Agency, Martin and her team coordinate complex events, recruit and manage teams, and develop business organization, management, and growth initiatives. Author of *How to Sizzle not Fizzle* (2015), Martin's editorial and project management skills have also resulted in several published works, including Tolle Lege Press's highly popular distribution of *The 1776 Project*. Martin resides in Metro Atlanta, where she wears many hats for a variety of business and political clients.